ANTHOLOGY
FOR
ASSEMBLY

ANTHOLOGY
FOR
ASSEMBLY

David Self

HUTCHINSON
London Melbourne Sydney Auckland Johannesburg

Hutchinson & Co. (Publishers) Ltd

An imprint of the Hutchinson Publishing Group
17–21 Conway Street, London W1P 6JD

Hutchinson Group (Australia) Pty Ltd
30–32 Cremorne Street, Richmond South, Victoria 3121
PO Box 151, Broadway, New South Wales 2007

Hutchinson Group (NZ) Ltd
32–34 View Road, PO Box 40–086, Glenfield, Auckland 10

Hutchinson Group (SA) (Pty) Ltd
PO Box 337, Bergvlei 2012, South Africa

First published 1982
Reprinted 1982, 1983 (twice)
© Selection and commentary David Self 1982

Set in VIP Palatino by
D. P. Media Limited, Hitchin, Hertfordshire

Printed and bound in Great Britain by
Anchor Brendon Ltd, Tiptree, Essex

ISBN 0 09 146900 7

Contents

Contents

Contents

Acknowledgements

The editor wishes to acknowledge his debt to the following in his compilation of this anthology:

The Reverend Geoffrey Curtis, David Geary, Geoffrey Marshall-Taylor, Ralph Rolls, Fiona Shore and the late Canon Peter Freeman; and also to Pat Herbert for her considerable help in the preparation of the typescript for the press.

The editor and publisher are grateful to the following copyright holders for permission to reproduce copyright material. Every effort has been made to trace owners of copyright material, but in some cases this has not proved possible. The publisher would be glad to hear from any others.

SCM Press Ltd for two excerpts from *School Worship: An Obituary* by John M. Hull

British Humanities Association for excerpt from *Wider Horizons* by James Hemming

Christian Education Movement for excerpt from Christian Education Movement paper 'The School Assembly'

The *Observer* for excerpts from Pendennis column; Tom Davies's report 'Welcome to Our World'

Christian Aid for excerpts from 'Clean Water: is it Too Much to Ask?' by Derrick Knight; 'A Question of Priorities'; 'Child Power'

William Collins Sons & Co. Ltd for excerpt from *Naught for Your Comfort* by Trevor Huddleston

Save the Children Fund for excerpt from 'The World's Children'

The *Sun* for 'Young People and Suicide' by Carolyn Martin

Raven Books Ltd for excerpt from *How to Make Friends* by Ivor Cutler

1

Michael Joseph Ltd for excerpt from *Walkabout* by James Vance Marshall

Geoffrey Bles Ltd for excerpts from *The Four Loves* by C.S. Lewis

National Youth Bureau for excerpt from 'The Samaritans and Young People' by Anthony Lawton

Darton, Longman & Todd Ltd for excerpt from *St Paul and his Epistles* by Hubert Richards

Penguin Books Ltd for excerpts from *Fables of Aesop*

Hodder & Stoughton Ltd for excerpt from *Reading, Writing and Relevance* by Mary Hoffman

William Collins Sons & Co. Ltd for excerpt from *Elidor* by Alan Garner

David Self for 'The Spiritual Healer'

Frank Graham for excerpts from 'Northumberland and Durham' by David Dougan and Frank Graham

Eastern Counties Newspapers Ltd for excerpt from 'Small Village Raises Big Sum'

Hodder & Stoughton Ltd for excerpts by John Hayter and Leonard Wilson from *John Leonard Wilson, Confessor for the Faith* by Roy McKay

Dr Edith Bone for excerpt from 'Seven Years in a Communist Gaol', BBC Radio

The *Catholic Herald* for excerpt from interview by Richard Dowden with Dr Sheila Cassidy

The Bodley Head for *Freedom to Breathe* by Alexander Solzhenitsyn, translated by Michael Glenny

A. Wheaton & Co. Ltd for excerpts from *In the Streets of Calcutta* by Audrey Constant; *God's Special Army* by Geoffrey Hanks

David Self for 'Elizabeth Fry'

The *Observer* Colour Magazine for excerpt from 'Churches in Torment' by Colin Cross

The Farmington Institute for excerpts from 'Thomas of Celano's First Life'

Hodder & Stoughton Ltd for *The Hiding Place* by Corrie ten Boom

BBC Publications for excerpt from *Richard Dimbleby: Broadcaster*

World Publishing Company for excerpts by Dr Hanaoka and Tom Stonier from *Nuclear Disaster* by Tom Stonier

The *Listener* for excerpt from 'Sacrifice of an Island' by Bob Friend

The Reverend Doctor Kenneth Greet for excerpt from letter about world disarmament

George Allen & Unwin for excerpt from 'The Five Loaves' from *Apocryphal Stories* by Karel Čapek

2

Taizé Community, 71250, France for excerpt from 'Second Letter to the People of God'

Lesley Davies for excerpt from 'My Brother's Keeper', broadcast in *Speak*, BBC Radio

David Self for 'Sorry!' from BBC 'Material for Secondary Assembly'

John P. Hogan for excerpt from 'Here and There' quoted in *Words for Worship*

Oxford University Press for excerpt from 'RUR' by Karel Čapek

Michael Joseph Ltd for excerpt from 'Compassion Circuit' from *Seeds of Time* by John Wyndham

Macdonald Educational Ltd for excerpt from *The Big Switch* by Muriel Box

Sidgwick & Jackson Ltd for excerpt from *The Machine Stops* by E.M. Forster

André Deutsch Ltd for excerpt from *Only One Earth* by Barbara Ward and René Dubois

Methuen & Co. Ltd for excerpt from *The Wind in the Willows* by Kenneth Grahame

Mark Vye for 'Prayer to the Car' published in *New Voices*

Methuen & Co. Ltd for excerpt from *I am David* by Anne Holm

The *Observer* Colour Magazine for excerpts from 'In the Synagogue' by Colin Cross; 'Creed for the Desert' by Colin Cross

The Leprosy Mission for excerpts from leaflets: 'Getting to Know About Leprosy' and '20 Questions about Leprosy'

The *Guardian* for excerpt from article about eczema by Christine Orton

Victor Gollancz for excerpt from *Annerton Pit* by Peter Dickinson

Lesley Davies for excerpt from 'Sympathy' broadcast in *Speak*, BBC Radio

Hamish Hamilton for 'The Glass in the Field' from *The Thurber Carnival* by James Thurber

Artia of Prahal for 'Unexpected Good Fortune' published in *Fairy Tale Tree*

William Collins Sons & Co. Ltd for excerpt from *The Phantom Tollbooth* by Norton Juster

Hamish Hamilton for *The Shore and the Sea* from *Further Fables for Our Time* by James Thurber

Evans Brothers Ltd for 'Genesis' by Brian Morris from *Things that Matter* edited by Philip Grosset

3

SCM Press Ltd for excerpts from *Getting and Spending* and *Working for a Living* by Jack Singleton

The Bodley Head for excerpt from 'Outside, Looking In' by Paul Jennings

Hodder & Stoughton Ltd for 'Money' from *Prayer for Pagans* by Roger Bush

Gill & Macmillan Ltd for excerpts from *Prayer Before a £5 Note* by Abbé Michel Quoist

Harrap & Co. Ltd for excerpt from *A Real Good Smile* by Bill Naughton

A. M. Heath for excerpt from *Escape from Childhood* by John Holt

Reader's Digest for 'Direct Wire' by Walter C. Mello, from *Getting the Best Out of Life*

James Watson for 'Mr William Hudson, JP'

David Self for 'Embarrassing Moments'

Lesley Davies for excerpts from 'In the Fashion', broadcast in *Speak*, BBC Radio

Yoga Today for article 'Get the Happiness Habit' by Heather Causnett

The *Guardian* for excerpt from article 'Turning the Table Manners' by Harry Whewell

Jonathan Cape Ltd for excerpt from *The Human Zoo* by Desmond Morris

Reader's Digest for excerpt from 'Keep Open the Windows of Your Mind' by Merle Crowell, from *Getting the Best Out of Life*

The *New York Times* for 'Letter to the President' signed Thomas Banyacya and others, on behalf of the Hopi people

SCM Press Ltd for excerpt from 'Letter from Prison' by Martin Luther King

Little, Brown & Co. for excerpt from 'The Cliché Expert', from *Sullivan at Bay* by Frank Sullivan; used by permission of the Historical Society of Saratoga Springs, N.Y.

The *Daily Mirror* for excerpt from 'The First Time' by Raymond Campbell

Sheed & Ward Ltd for excerpt from *Before the Living God* by Ruth Burrows

The *Guardian* for excerpt from article on Muslim wives by Polly Toynbee

Wildwood House Ltd for excerpt from *Birth Without Violence* by Frederic Leboyer

4

Puffin Books Ltd for excerpt from *The Freedom Tree* by James Watson

Consumers' Association for excerpt from 'What to do when Someone Dies'

Cambridge YMCA for excerpt from 'The View from the Hearse' by Reverend John Mason

Allen & Unwin Ltd for excerpt from *The Autobiography of Bertrand Russell* by Bertrand Russell

Sidgwick & Jackson Ltd for excerpt from 'Mr Andrews' by E.M. Forster, from *The Eternal Moment*

Routledge & Kegan Paul Ltd for excerpt from *This is Your Child* by Anne Allen and Arthur Morton

David Self for 'Why Suffering? The Buddhist Answer', 'Prometheus'; 'The Story of Job'

Allen & Unwin Ltd for excerpt from *My Life and Thoughts* by Albert Schweitzer

David Self for 'Hinduism'

The *Observer* for excerpt from 'How to be a Hajj'

The *Observer* Colour Magazine for excerpt from 'How the Militant Sikhs All Came to be Known as Lions', from *Religion with No Food* by Colin Cress

The *Observer* for excerpts from 'The Roots of the Rastas' by James Fox

Hutchinson Education for excerpt from *Who am I?* by Martin Ballard

Faber & Faber Ltd for excerpt from *Country Days* by A. G. Street

National Christian Education Council for excerpt from 'Search for Meaning 4 – Who is My Neighbour?' by Raymond Trudgian

The Hogarth Press Ltd for excerpt from *Cider with Rosie* by Laurie Lee

The Royal British Legion for excerpt from 'How it all Began'; 'Fact Sheets'

David Self for 'Christmas Preparations'

Oxford University Press for excerpt from *The Story of the Elizabethan Actors* by Katherine Hudson

BBC Publications for excerpt from *Contact* written by Geoffrey Marshall-Taylor

The *Catholic Herald* for excerpt from 'Christmas in Nazareth'

The *Observer* for excerpts from 'Black Christmas, White Christians' by Colin Cross

Aberdeen University for 'Santa's Clauses', from *The Meretricious Muse* by C.A. McLaren and W.J.S. Kirton

The *Observer* for 'Epiphany' by Colin Cross

B.T. Batsford Ltd for excerpt from *The Folklore of East Anglia* by Enid Porter

The *Observer* for excerpt from 'St Pauls and the Visions that Changed the World' by Colin Cross

Ward Lock Educational Co. Ltd for excerpts from *Roman Catholicism* by Peter Kelly

Church Information Office for excerpt from *This Church of England* by David L. Edwards. Reproduced from *This Church of England* (CIO Publishing, 1962) by kind permission of the Central Board of Finance of the Church of England

A.D. Peters & Co. for excerpts from 'Mother and Son' by Liam O'Flaherty, from *The Short Stories of Liam*

Lutterworth Press for excerpt from *Judaism* by Myer Domnitz

Geoffrey Bles Ltd for excerpts from *The Lion, the Witch and the Wardrobe* by C.S. Lewis

William Collins Sons & Co. Ltd for excerpts from *Jesus of Nazareth* by William Barclay

The *Observer* for excerpt from 'Rome Versus Rex'

Victor Gollancz Ltd for excerpt from *Let's go to Golgotha* by Garry Kilworth

SCM Press Ltd for excerpt from *A New People's Life of Christ* by William Barclay

Faber & Faber Ltd for excerpt from *The Davidson Affair* by Stuart Jackman

Ward Lock Educational Co. Ltd for excerpt from *The Orthodox Church* by Sergei Hackel

The editors of Time-Life Books for excerpt from Life World Library, *Greece* by Alexander Eliot

Tor Mark Press for excerpt from *Cornish Customs and Superstitions* by Robert Hunt

Hodder & Stoughton Ltd for excerpt from 'The Epistles' from *Prayer Book Commentaries* by Reverend A.M. Stibbs

The *Observer* Colour Magazine for excerpts from 'Creed from the Desert' by Colin Cross; 'The Greatest Journey in the World' by Brian Moyhahan

The *Observer* for excerpt from 'Mecca – Inside the Pilgrim City' by Patrick Seal

Harvey Unna & Stephen Durbridge Ltd for 'A Lad on the Tyneside' by Leonard Barras

Church Information Office for 'The Lord's Prayer'. 'The Lord's Prayer' from the Alternative Service Book, 1980 is the copyright of the International Consultation on English Texts and is reproduced by permission of the Central Board of Finance of the Church of England

Sidgwick & Jackson for *The Wonder that was India* translated by A.J. Bashai

INTRODUCTION

Many of us can tell horror stories about school assemblies; stories such as the one about the teacher who was seen to clout an inattentive boy round the ears between verses one and two of 'Jesus friend of little children'; or the headteacher who told his school that, while they were singing in praise of God's creation, they were to look at him and not out of the window.

It seems the wrong moments always prove the most memorable. Indeed the assembly that stays most vividly in my mind from my own schooldays is the one that climaxed in the apparent prayer, 'And if you must smoke on the way home from school, then for God's sake take your caps off first.' For months I equated smoking with entering a church: both activities required you to remove your hat. In fact worship and the maintenance of discipline are often uncomfortable neighbours in assembly: 'It's the beginning of a new term. I want to have a happy term, and I want you to have a happy term, and Jesus wants you to have a happy term but I won't have a happy term and you won't have a happy term and Jesus won't have a happy term if you climb on the toilet roof.'

Many of these infelicities result from the need to give out notices while trying to implement the famous 1944 Education Act which talked about the daily 'act of worship' with which each school day should begin, and in which the whole school community should participate. The frequent result of these two conflicting demands has been the traditional recipe of a story, a hymn and a prayer (the story usually being from the Bible), immediately followed by 'announcements' which unfortunately are often more interesting and more relevant than anything that has gone before. This format has its critics ('It's boring', 'It's always the same') and its supporters: 'If they don't get the Bible in

9

school, where will they get it?' 'They know where they are with this pattern'. (Or more thruthfully, *'We* know where *we* are with this pattern'.)

Since the late sixties styles have changed and morning assembly is now just as likely to feature a pop group, a film or slide show, or a visiting speaker. Most frequently it includes a reading that is intended to possess the magical qualities of relevance, impact and uplift; and it is to help those who must find a steady supply of such material that this anthology has been compiled.

Such a collection of source material is not the place to debate the nature and philosophy of the school assembly, but it may be helpful to point out that there is a difference between an assembly and an act of worship. A British Humanist Association booklet, *Wider Horizons*, defines the purpose of an assembly thus: 'The purpose of assembly in a secondary school, from a social and psychological point of view, is to 'celebrate' the values that are recognized as fundamental to wholeness and richness in personal and social life – the civilized and civilizing values.'

A Christian Education Movement paper on the school assembly draws the distinction between such assemblies and acts of worship.

All can take part in an assembly as here described but if the adults or the children who plan the assembly introduce explicit religious references, through the material used, explanation, discussion or the introduction of hymns or prayers, then the intention changes . . . and if the assembly thus begins to take the traditional form of Christian worship, then difficulties may arise.

It would seem that the basic problem of the attendance of children and teacher at a regular act of worship is that it is held to imply commitment and for some this would seem insincere or dishonest.

As a Christian, I would number myself among this latter group. I have no wish to involve young people in a pretence of worship. Equally this does not mean that I believe religion should be excluded from assembly. Such gatherings can be suitable places to hear about the world faiths, about our own traditions and culture, and those of other peoples. Indeed, when it comes to stating the aims of the school assembly, I cannot do better than quote Dr John M. Hull's admirably sane book, *School Worship: An Obituary* (London: SCM Press, 1975):

10

1   To widen the pupil's repertoire of appropriate emotional response. An appropriate emotional response is one which in terms of the surrounding society is proportioned to the circumstances which evoke it. A person who flies into a fury if he loses his fountain pen but is unmoved by the human need in the great city around him has inappropriate emotions. A person who is not moved by the beautiful and who never feels compassion is lacking in emotional breadth.

2   To encourage a reflective approach to living, a way which transcends the immediacy of experience. Man's capacity for reflection upon himself and his worth is part of his distinctive existence.

3   To demonstrate the values which are not controversial and upon which democratic society depends. These values include freedom of speech, respect for the rights of minorities, the equality before the law and in education of all religious and ethnic groups, and responsibility for personal decision-making and for participation in community decision-making.

4   To provide some experience and understanding of what worship is so that the way of worship, along with other life styles, will remain an option for anyone who wishes to follow it and so that all will have some insight into what it is like to live a religious life. But this provision will not require any one to worship and will certainly not commit the school to corporate acts of worship.

Consequently this anthology includes several passages *about* religious topics. References to Biblical passages are also provided where such passages may be naturally read in conjunction with specific readings, though such references are by no means exhaustive and many others will suggest themselves to the user of this book.

Additionally, a number of well-known prayers have been included at the back of the book for use where appropriate. To quote Dr Hull again:

It is wholly appropriate that when a priest or layman has been leading a series of assemblies, he should conclude with the words: 'I am going to pray a prayer much loved by my fellow believers. I hope you will enjoy listening to it.' Since it does not commit the listeners and does not purport to represent anything other than the views of the speaker and his co-religionists, such a procedure seems quite unobjectionable. Indeed, it is often found that such prayers are listened to with rather more interest and respect than it usually the case in school assembly.

11

The prayers have been quoted in their best known forms. Some users may wish to adapt them – for example, altering 'thou' and 'thy' to 'you' and 'your' etc.

Like the prayers, the passages will not all be suitable for use in every situation. Assemblies cannot be pre-packaged for use in all circumstances and the user of this material must be selective (and also adapt introductions to meet local needs).

However, my experience over ten years as a teacher responsible for school assembly has taught me what is likely to work with possibly indifferent (or even hostile) audiences. Subsequently as one-time producer of, and as regular contributor to, the BBC School Radio series *Material for Assembly* and *Impact*, I have become aware of the varying demands of different school situations. Additionally, as the compiler and presenter of a hundred editions of Anglia Television's late night religious *Anthology* programme I have learnt the necessity of selecting only passages which have a wide and immediate appeal.

The passages in this book have all been thoroughly 'tested' in one or other of the above situations. They are arranged thematically in groups of five, and a particular sequence of readings may therefore be used daily during the course of a week. In almost every case, these passages can also be used individually and out of sequence. Also included are a number of seasonal readings for use as required.

I have chosen those passages which read naturally even in larger assemblies and I have not included anything I would be embarrassed to stand up and read aloud myself. I have let the writers' voices be heard unadapted, rather than re-writing their work in some kind of bland prose that is less demanding on the reader. Rehearsal is advised before any reading, and some thought should be given as to who is the best available reader (or readers) for any particular passage.

The gathering together of a large number of people for any assembly places a heavy responsibility on those in charge of that assembly. I hope that this collection of material will be of some help to those who bear that responsibility (and indeed to all religious education, social studies and English teachers). In the end though, it is the assembly leader's own judgement, preparation and sincerity that must make any material or subject acceptable and memorable – for the right reasons.

THEMES

1

Those in need

---•◦•◦•◦•----

1: THE BOAT PEOPLE

In recent years, many refugees have left Vietnam by boat in the hope of reaching a free country. In 1980, an Observer *journalist, Tom Davies, set out from Hong Kong on a police launch, captained by Les Bird and in the company of an Australian writer, Norman MacSwan. Many of the boats they found were flimsy in the extreme. The refugees suffered much else besides.*

'Everything is against them,' says Les Bird. 'They've been driven out of their homes at gunpoint. If the typhoons don't get them there's Thai pirates. There's barracudas and sharks in these waters and I once picked up one who'd had his leg bitten off in the sea.'

The police launch had been at sea for only a short while when a boat was sighted.

As we approach the thin bobbing craft it's a sight which shatters your heart. There are thirteen on board with a sail made out of a patchwork of every sort of material. Two of them are feverishly bailing water out of the hold while, under a tarpaulin, a mother sits holding two brown, sleeping babies, one with a terrible rash.

Their eyes are wide and worried as they look up at us. They haven't a clue what is going to happen to them. For all they know we are going to open fire since our vessel is heavily and visibly armed.

One man has a lampshade for a hat. Planks are riddled with rot. Their clothes are ragged, though, says Les Bird, they're not as badly fed as many he's taken in.

The women have full beautiful mouths and lie on their backs on

15

the deck, hands on foreheads, clearly exhausted. Two small boys are asleep and curled up under a sack.

A man is standing holding the tiller and I go down and say, 'Welcome to the Free World your grace'. He doesn't understand a word and looks worried until I stuff a large Havana cigar in his mouth. He lights it himself, looks at it, holds up his head and laughs with all the jubilation in the world in his throat.

Everyone begins laughing and clapping as we hand out bottles of beer and cigars. They've done it, they've made it and they're not going to get shot. The women utter great golden gales of chuckles from their mouths. The joy is unconfined. After that trip everything can now only get better.

Norman and I look at each other and there are tears running down our faces. 'Australians aren't supposed to cry,' I say and, always great at covering up inner feelings with a joke, he replies, 'It's not them that's making me cry. It's all this beer we're giving away.'

They take the tops of the beer bottles with their teeth and you note they are busy sharing it amongst themselves. It is a spirit of mutual self-help which has brought them through one of the most fearful journeys known to man. Everywhere the continual eruption of laughter.

Tom Davies

2: TOO MUCH TO ASK?

In Britain, and throughout the developed world, fresh water is used as if there were no tomorrow. A family uses on average from twenty-two to sixty gallons a day. A couple of gallons go to wash a few cups. The tea leaves go down the lavatory pan with three gallons more. We wash a child's hands under a running tap and a gallon and a half disappears down the drain. A car wash takes a minimum of twenty-five gallons, an automatic household washing machine can use over sixty gallons to complete a cycle of operations for one nine pound load of dry washing.

According to World Health Organization figures, in 1975, 1233 million people in the Third World (excluding China) had no adequate clean water. In 1980 the figure was 1730 million. Put another way it means that some three out of five people alive today in the developing countries have no easy access to safe drinking water. Three out of four persons in these same countries have no kind of sanitary facilities.

This report comes from a Christian Aid News *reporter in Peru.*

A year ago I was in Chimbote, a Peruvian fishing port which grew fast during the anchovy boom of the sixties and virtually died when the local stocks of fish were too greedily harvested to supply the fishmeal needs of Europe and North America. Chimbote is now a town without a heart, suffering massive unemployment and deprivation. The people are hungry.

Most of its population squat in barriadas (shanty towns) of wood and strawmat on the sand dunes above the town. In this part of Peru it seldom rains. My guide was a young priest with some medical training, Father Alonso. This is what he told me as we stood in a muddle of straw shacks.

'Only last night a young mother came to me carrying a dying child – dying of malnutrition caused by severe diarrhoea. "How many other children have you?" I asked.

' "Five," she replied, "but three died of malnutrition." "How is that possible?" I exclaimed, to which she answered: "It was God's will."

'What could I say to her in her agony? The problem of diarrhoea in this community is a problem of drinking water. There is none available at a price the poor can afford and so small children drink polluted water, fall sick and die.

'And we ask the parents, is it normal that the children die? Who wills it? Is it God's will? No, it is not, we say emphatically. Religion plays a very important part in these people's lives. Is it a matter of luck or of destiny? We also ask. But the answer is again, no. Children die because of the abnormal social conditions in which they live. They die because of the lack of money, lack of water, lack of drainage.'

A water lorry, peddling water by the gallon comes up the hill. Alonso looks on sadly.

'This is just one way in which the poor are exploited,' he says. 'In this barriada, there is no drinking water, no standpipe. Down in the town there is a standing charge for a tap in one's own house which costs seventy soles (twenty pence) a month and you can use all the water you can take. The water lorry men fill up at their own taps and come up here and sell their own water by the can at a high profit. These poor people cannot afford it but they cannot do without it either.'

Similar stories could be found in many parts of the world. Diarrhoea directly kills six million children in the developing countries every year. Diarrhoea and malnutrition form a vicious circle in which one reinforces the other. In India alone, one and a half million children under five die of diarrhoeal diseases every year.

If everyone in the world had access to safe drinking water and sanitation, infant mortality could be cut by as much as fifty per cent world-wide.

Derrick Knight

A great deal has been done in recent years to improve water supplies and organize systems of sanitation in the Third World. International aid has provided finance and voluntary agencies like Christian Aid have played their part. But the scale of the problem is enormous and the world population is rising faster than the provision of facilities. That is why the United Nations and its family of specialized agencies have launched The International Drinking Water Supply and Sanitation Decade with its slogan: 'Fresh water for all by 1990'.

3: JACOB LEDWABA

People in need may lack other things besides food and water and medicine. This is the story of a black South African who died because he forgot to carry his pass with him.

The story-teller is Bishop Trevor Huddleston who, at the time of the event, was a priest working in the black township of Sophiatown, outside Johannesburg.

Jacob Ledwaba worked in a milk-bar managed by a white man. On the Saturday before Easter, Jacob failed to come to work, and the manager came to see Father Huddleston. He was angry.

'It's Jacob . . .' he began . . . 'Father, I'm damn well going to do something about this . . . it's a bloody shame . . . Father, you've got to help me. . . .'

On Maundy Thursday night at Jeppe station, Jacob Ledwaba had been arrested for being out after the curfew and without his pass. On Saturday morning he came home. He told his wife he had been kicked in the stomach in the cells and that he was in such pain that he couldn't go to work. Would she go and tell the boss, and explain? It was this that brought the manager of the milk bar to my office at the Mission on Holy Saturday morning.

It would be easy to dramatize this incident – and in many recent novels on South Africa such incidents have been described. All I

want to say is this. Jacob was taken to hospital and died of a
bladder injury, leaving a widow and a month-old baby. We
brought a case against the police, and in evidence produced
affidavits concerning the nature of the injury from the two doctors who had attended Jacob. We also had the services of an
eminent Q.C.

The verdict (long after Jacob's body had been laid in the cemetery: long after any fresh medical evidence could possibly come to
light) was that he had died of congenital syphilis. The magistrate
added a rider to his verdict to the effect that the police had been
shamefully misrepresented in this case, and that there was no
evidence whatever inculpating them.

So Jacob died, in the first place because he had forgotten to
carry his pass. In the second because, Good Friday being a public
holiday in South Africa, he had spent twenty-four hours in the
police cells in Jeppe.

This thing happened quite a long time ago now, and I suppose
that if Jacob's son is still alive he is just at the beginning of his
schooldays. It will only be a few years more till the day when he,
too, must carry a pass. I only hope and pray he will not be so
careless as his father was, and forget it one evening when he goes
to visit his friends. It can be very costly to forget your pass.

Trevor Huddleston

4: THE EMPTY COFFIN

*This report is from a Save the Children Fund medical team working in
Guatemala. (Save the Children Week is usually held in late April or early
May. The address of the Society is Jebb House, 157 Clapham Road,
London SW9 0PT.)*

Dr Effrain Lopez Juarez was unwinding after an exhausting day
dealing with the health problems at Joyabaj – a large agricultural
area of Guatemala where Save the Children have a team.

He was looking forward to a quiet evening when suddenly
there was a tap on the door. . . . It was Nancy Lorence, the
Fund's Education Programme Director. On her way back from a
trip to a mountain village she had passed through the village of
Caquil, where she was told a little girl was dying.

She tried to persuade the parents to let her take their daughter

19

to the town's health centre for treatment – but they refused. They
wanted her to die at home, they said.

'I decided to go to the village to see if the child could be saved
and set out in the land-rover with two volunteers from the
Joyabaj emergency ambulance service, Hector and Elmer, our
accountant.

Approaching the village which is about ten miles from the
town we could see the flaming torches moving towards the
child's house and we thought that this meant she was probably
already dead.

But the child was still breathing when we got there, though
barely – a pretty little two-year-old who, at first glance, seemed
half-asleep. She had a high fever and did not respond. While I
gave her first aid her grandmother told us how the child had been
ill for two weeks with diarrhoea and vomiting.

After a long struggle we convinced the parents that there was a
chance of saving her. They agreed to come with us to the health
centre. It was staffed only by a nurse at that time of night so we
stayed with the child. Although she was severely ill and very
weak she had a strong will to live. She continued to fight even
when, at 3 a.m. she began to vomit blood and her breathing
became even more difficult.

We continued the treatment for two days until she began to
improve and asked for something to eat. Three days later she was
well enough to return home.

The family is happily complete again. But the father is still
wondering what to do with the coffin he bought for his little girl
on the night we were called.'

5: YOUNG PEOPLE AND SUICIDE

This passage is part of a feature published in the Sun *in 1977. It is
included so that students can have their attention drawn to the Samaritans, and it is strongly suggested that a Samaritan be invited to talk to
the school assembly. (See also page 25.)*

Jane, an only child, was sixteen when she rebelled against her
family. She left their comfortable house in South London for a
squat in Paddington.

Her father, a bank official, and her mother, a community
worker, were upset and bewildered when Jane suddenly decided

to leave school and abandoned her A levels. She was a swot at school, and kept herself apart from her class-mates.

Jane was attracted to the squatting community as a complete contrast to her neat suburban life. She believed that doing her own thing was what she really wanted.

She says, 'When I saw people my own age living with absolute freedom in what appeared to be an idyllic community, when I visited there before, I thought candles for light and paraffin lamps for heat were very back-to-nature. It wasn't until I had to live that way all the time that I realized how pleasant suburban central heating can be. Small things, like not being able to wash your hair if you felt like it, all piled up, I suppose.'

Jane spent most of the day just hanging about the squat, becoming more and more depressed.

So she went to the doctor for some sleeping pills, came home and swallowed the lot. Another girl found her in time to be treated in hospital and survive.

A social worker eventually helped Jane to return to her family. She has gone back to college and, for the first time in years, began to communicate with her parents.

Carolyn Martin

Every hour, a teenager in Britain picks up a telephone in desperation and threatens suicide.

Susan Flint, assistant director of the Samaritans' London branch, says: 'You can't just dismiss these threats as attention-seeking gestures. There's only one cheerful point about all this. Young people are attempting to talk about their problems more than before. We give a lot of talks in schools. Often we can persuade children to see someone. That's when we can start getting to the root of their problems.'

The joint general secretary of the Samaritans gives this advice: 'If you are feeling really depressed, ring us. You'll find the Samaritans' number in your local telephone directory. There are over 160 branches in the British Isles.

'You can come in to talk to us or, if you are so depressed that you don't want to go out, we have a flying squad of two people from each branch who will come to see you.'

2
Friendship

1: HOW TO MAKE FRIENDS

First of all, take a large bucket of whitewash, then stand by the window and look out. When you see someone approaching whom you would like to know, wait until he is directly below, then empty the bucket over his head.

He will stop, and look up, and shout unspeakable language at you. You will reply, 'Do come upstairs and clean yourself up' and throw him down the key.

He will pick up your key and enter your home, tramping whitewash into the carpet all the way up.

You will say, 'Come. Have a bath,' light the geyser and start running the water. He will take his clothes off, and as he is taking them off say, 'Ah! You have a hole in your underwear. Let me mend it while you are having your bath.' He will say, 'Thank you. I am very grateful for this'.

While he is in the bath, sit there talking to him, darning his vest. It doesn't matter what kind of thread you use, it is the deed which is important. I myself use cobbler's thread, because when he wears the vest and feels the cobbler's thread against his skin, it is a constant reminder to him of our friendship and he thinks, 'I must phone this man again'.

When he is dry, and in your best red silk dressing-gown, with the dragons, then he can take his clothes, put them into the bath water and wash them, then hang them out of the window to dry.

Say to him, 'Come and sit with me and talk to me by the window while they are drying.' Then you talk, enjoying one another's conversation.

By this time the clothes are dry. Fetch them in and he will don them, thanking you for the darn of his vest.

And it is now lunch, you offer him a share of your dinner.

After dinner he says, 'Well, I really must go now,' and as you go downstairs he notices with alarm the whitewash on the carpet and says, 'Goodness! Look what I have done to your carpet.' And you say, 'No, I only rent a room here. It is the landlord's carpet.' Then he says,' We cannot let you get into bad odour with the landlord. Let us together clean the carpet.' So you clean the carpet, and this makes your friendship stronger than ever.

When you have cleaned the carpet, he says, 'Well, I really must go now, but I shall come and see you again tomorrow and we shall have another long talk.'

You have made a friend.

Ivor Cutler

2: THE SNEEZE

This reading is about another way of making friends. It comes from a novel called Walkabout *by James Vance Marshall which tells of a teenage girl, Mary, and her young brother Peter who are the only survivors of an aircrash in the Australian outback.*

After wandering through the desert, Mary and Peter suddenly come face to face with an Aborigine boy. The three children stand looking at each other in the middle of the Australian desert. At first Mary is afraid.

Mary had decided not to move. To move would be a sign of weakness. She remembered being told about the man who'd come face to face with a lion, and had stared it out, had caused it to slink discomfited away. That was what she'd do to the black boy; she'd stare at him until he felt the shame of his nakedness and slunk away. She thrust out her chin, and glared.

After a while Peter started to fidget. The delay was fraying his nerves. He wished someone would do something: wished something would happen. Then, quite involuntarily, he himself started a new train of events. His hand began to waggle; his nose tilted skywards; he spluttered and choked; he tried to hold his breath; but all in vain. It had to come. He sneezed. . . .

To his sister the sneeze was a calamity. . . . She had just intensified her stare to the point – she felt sure – of irresistibility, when the spell was shattered. The bush boy's attention shifted from her to Peter. Frustration warped her sense of justice. She condemned her brother out of court; was turning on him angrily, when a second sneeze, even mightier than the first, shattered the silence of the bush.

Mary raised her eyes to heaven: invoking the gods as witnesses to her despair. But the vehemence of the second sneeze was still tumbling leaves from the humble-bushes, when a new sound made her whirl around. A gust of laughter: melodious laughter; low at first, then becoming louder, unrestrained, disproportionate, uncontrolled.

She looked at the bush boy in amazement. He was doubled up with belly-shaking spasms of mirth.

Peter's incongruous, out-of-proportion sneeze had touched off one of his peoples' most highly developed traits: a sense of the ridiculous; a sense so keenly felt as to be almost beyond control. The bush boy laughed with complete abandon. He flung himself to the ground. He rolled head-over-heels in unrestrained delight.

His mirth was infectious. At first apologetically, then whole-heartedly, Peter too started to laugh.

The barrier of twenty thousand years vanished in the twinkling of an eye.

James Vance Marshall

3: FRIENDS AND COMPANIONS

How do two people become friends? C.S. Lewis believes friendship begins to grow when two people have similar interests.

Long before history began men have got together apart from the women and done things. We had to. And to like doing what must be done is a characteristic that has survival value. We not only had to do the things, we had to talk about them. We had to plan the hunt and the battle. When they were over we had to hold a post-mortem and draw conclusions for future use. We liked this even better. We ridiculed or punished the cowards and bunglers, we praised the star-performers. We revelled in technicalities. ('He might have known he'd never get near the brute, not with the wind that way' . . . 'You see, I had a lighter arrowhead; that's what did it' . . . 'What I always say is –' . . . 'Stuck him just like that, see? Just the way I'm holding this stick' . . .) In fact, we talked shop. We enjoyed one another's society greatly we Braves, we hunters, all bound together by shared skill, shared dangers and hardships, esoteric jokes – away from the women and children.

What were the women doing meanwhile? Well, they certainly often had rituals from which men were excluded. When, as sometimes happened, agriculture was in their hands, they must, like the men, have had common skills, toils and triumphs. Yet perhaps their world was never as emphatically feminine as that of their men-folk was masculine. The children were with them; perhaps the old men were there, too.

This pleasure in co-operation, in talking shop, in the mutual respect and understanding of men who daily see one another tested, is biologically valuable. You may, if you like, regard it as 'instinct'.

This Companionship is often called Friendship, and many people when they speak of their 'friends' mean only their companions.

But what then is real Friendship? Is it more than Companionship?

Real Friendship arises out of this Companionship when two or more of the companions discover that they have in common some insight or interest or even taste which the others do not share and which, till that moment, each believed to be his own unique treasure (or burden). The typical expression of opening Friendship would be something like, 'What? You too?' We can imagine that among those early hunters and warriors single individuals saw what others did not; saw that the deer was beautiful as well as edible, that hunting was fun as well as necessary, dreamed that his gods might be not only powerful but holy. It is when two such persons discover one another – it is then that true Friendship is born.

C.S. Lewis

4: THE SAMARITANS

Who are the Samaritans? What do they do? How do they offer 'friendship'? (See also page 20.)

Not all of us have friends we can talk to when we are troubled, and sometimes the friends and relations we could talk to are not there when we need them. There are occasions when you want to talk about something too personal to tell friends or family and want to be sure no one knows what you are doing. You may even want to talk *about* your friends or family.

The Samaritans offer someone who will act like a friend to whom you can talk at any time of the day or night at each of the 160 centres in Britain and Ireland. The most important aspect of this is listening to whatever the caller wants to talk about, and *helping* the caller to talk about how they feel, what is going wrong, and what can be done. Sometimes just talking things out is enough. At other times decisions may have to be made. Although the Samaritans are 'right behind you' they never tell you what to do; they try to help you calm down and decide for yourself. This is not always achieved in one meeting or one telephone conversation; it may be over weeks or even months of contact.

Everything told to the Samaritans is totally confidential; nothing is said to parents or friends, to husbands or wives or lovers, to the police, to doctors or social workers; nothing to anybody unless the caller wants something said. This is why so many people feel it is safe to tell the Samaritans very personal things and this feeling of safety is increased for some people because they do not even have to give a name. Other people prefer to give at least a christian name, and some prefer a face-to-face meeting, although it is with a total stranger, because it is easier to talk to a stranger than to someone you know.

It doesn't matter how old or young you are, or what you are calling about, the Samaritans never try and persuade you to do anything. They believe that the best way to help someone is to help him sort things out for himself, and whatever his age he can be responsible if he is allowed to be so. After all, the person who knows best how he feels is the person in trouble.

Anthony Lawton

5: A POSTCARD TO PHILEMON

One of the most attractive pictures of friendship in the Bible is Paul's short Epistle to Philemon. It is here introduced by Hubert Richards, an author and lecturer in religious studies.

One of the letters Paul wrote is now known as the Epistle to

Philemon. 'Epistle' is a rather grandiose name for what is really little more than a postcard.

Philemon was one of the outstanding citizens in the town of Colossae, and he had become a Christian under the influence of Paul's preaching there. Towards the end of his life Paul wrote to the Christians in Colossae from his prison in Rome, and took the opportunity to put this private note to Philemon in the same post. Its survival in the New Testament is possibly due to the fact that Philemon was the first to make a full collection of Paul's letters, and included this personal letter at the end of the collection. Certainly the fact that he published it suggests that it made a deep impression on him.

At Colossae, Philemon had owned a pagan slave named Onesimos*. The name means 'useful', and since the word is twice used in the letter as a pun, a modern translation would have to render it with something like 'Andy'. In any case Onesimos had proved rather useless: he had stolen Philemon's savings and made off to Rome, hoping like many thieves since to get lost in the 'smoke'.

He had not reckoned with the fact that Paul was in Rome at the time and, house-prisoner though he was, Paul not only established contact with him but made a Christian of him too. 'In fact,' he tells Philemon, 'he's been most handy to me because he's been able to run errands for me round the town while I've been housebound.'

However, there is no question of Onesimos staying in Rome in Paul's service. Paul has no right to keep him; he is still Philemon's property, and if Philemon wants to apply the full rigour of the current law on robbery he can have him put to death. As Paul packs off the slave to his master, his covering note simply asks Philemon to consider the situation carefully. Onesimos is still technically his slave, but in Christ Jesus he has also become his brother.

The Epistle to Philemon *is effectively rendered by Alan Dale in* New World, *his translation of the New Testament, published by the Oxford University Press.*

---

* Onesimos is pronounced O – ne – si – mos.

3
Aesop's Fables

There is authority for the existence of Aesop, but very little is known about him for certain. He is thought to have lived in Greece in the sixth century B.C. and is said to have been a slave and to have been killed by the people of Delphi when they threw him off a mountain top because they did not like the morals of his stories.

His fables are drawn from a variety of sources, and three-quarters of them are about animals. These five however concern humans but, like the others, are anecdotes on which is hung a moral lesson or piece of sensible advice.

1: CRYING WOLF

There was a shepherd who was fond of playing practical jokes. He would drive his flock some distance from the village and then shout to the villagers for help, saying that wolves had attacked his sheep. Two or three times the inhabitants came rushing out in alarm – and then went back with the shepherd laughing at them.

Eventually, however, some wolves really came. They got between the shepherd and his flock and he called the neighbours to aid him. But they thought he was up to his usual trick and did not bother their heads about him. So he lost his sheep.

The moral: A scaremonger gains nothing by raising false alarms. He merely makes people disbelieve him when he does speak the truth.

2: A FRIEND IN NEED

Two friends were travelling together when a bear suddenly appeared. One of them climbed up a tree in time and remained there hidden. The other, seeing that he would be caught in

28

another moment, lay down on the ground and pretended to be dead. When the bear put its muzzle to him and smelt him all over, he held his breath – for it is said that a bear will not touch a corpse.

After it had gone away, the other man came down from his tree and asked his friend what the bear had whispered in his ear. 'It told me,' he replied, 'not to travel in future with friends who do not stand by one in peril.'

The moral: Genuine friends are proved by adversity.

3: SHARE AND SHARE ALIKE

Two men were journeying together when one of them noticed an axe lying on the ground. 'We have had a lucky find,' said his companion. 'Don't say "We", replied the other, 'say "You have had a find".'

Shortly afterwards the people who had lost the axe came up with them, and the man who had it, seeing the owners in pursuit, said, 'We are done for.'

'Don't say "We", ' his companion answered, 'say "I am done for" – since when you found the axe you would not let me share possession of it.'

The moral: If we do not give our friends a share of our good fortune, they will not be faithful to us in adversity.

4: WHERE YOUR TREASURE IS . . .

A miser sold all his possessions, made an ingot of the gold that he got for them, and hid it in a certain spot, where his own heart and thoughts were buried with it. Every day he came to gloat over his treasure. A labourer who had watched him guessed his secret, dug up the gold and carried it away; and when the miser came and found the hole empty he began to lament and pluck out his hair. A passer-by who saw him inquired the cause of his grief, and said: 'Do not be downcast, sir. Even when you had the gold you might as well not have had it. Take a stone instead and put it in the earth, and imagine that you have the gold there. That will serve the same purpose. For as far as I can see, even when it was there you did not make any use of the gold that you possessed.'

The moral: Possession without enjoyment is nothing.

5: SEEING IS BELIEVING

An athlete was always being called a weakling by his compat-riots. So he went abroad for a time; and on his return he boasted of the many feats he had performed in various countries, and especially of a jump which he had made at Rhodes – a jump such as no Olympic victor could equal.

'I can prove it by the testimony of eye-witnesses,' he said, 'if any of the people who were present ever come here.'

At this one of the bystanders said, 'If what you say is true, my man, you don't need witnesses. The place where you stand will do as well as Rhodes. Let us see the jump.'

The moral: The point of this story is that it is a waste of words to talk about something which can easily be put to the proof.

4

Getting things done

1: UNDERGROUND ACTIVITIES

This remarkable project was undertaken by pupils at a special school for physically handicapped children in north London. The children were taken to and from school in special buses throughout their school years. Some of the pupils in their last year had begun to worry about how to cope with travelling around London, as they contemplated what jobs they would be able to apply for. It emerged in discussion on transport that some members of the group had never travelled on the London Underground.

The aim of the project was to find out how accessible the London Underground system was to physically handicapped people. Before the children started, their teacher visited London Transport officials at a main line station and met their legal representative. She discovered from them that there was no document already in existence which was equivalent to the one her pupils were planning to compile. In addition she was informed that only one station had a ramp and that very few stations now had lifts; this meant that the pupils would not be able to take wheel-chairs. There was only one member of the group who was dependent on a chair, so he was given the task of processing material already supplied by London Transport. Most of the information received had been organized on the basis of the different Underground lines. The boy in the wheel-chair began to reorganize this into alphabetical order of stations.

The rest of the group chose a sample of the stations to check accessibility factors such as levels, ramps, escalators, lifts; they chose to check different facilities on each line. They would set off from the Underground station nearest to the school and travel to

31

their chosen destination, where they were sometimes met and escorted by a station official. For each visit, a group leader volunteered to get the rest of the class to their destination. It was the job of that day's leader to make sure that they all took the correct route and adjust any mistakes made in the course of the journey. Each visit was preceded by a class discussion using a tube map, so that routes and changes were planned beforehand and all the children, as well as the day's leader, were given practice in map-reading and diagrammatic conventions.

Time was the greatest problem for this handicapped group, as they had to work within the school curriculum. They had no mishaps or accidents, although several children had walking aids of some kind and many of these had not used the Underground before. The children did not conduct their survey during rush-hours, but the confidence they gained in travelling was more likely to help them when eventually faced with a more crowded situation.

Mary Hoffman

The guide was later published by the Central Council for the Disabled and has proved helpful to many other disabled people.

2: THE DOOR

This is a fictitious story about the power of the mind; how mind can overcome matter. A boy called Roland, guided by a priest-like man called Malebron, finds his way to a mysterious kingdom that is buried under a smooth grassy mound.

'How do we get in?' said Roland.
'Through the door,' replied Malebron.
'What door? It's just turf.'
'That is why you are here,' said Malebron. 'The door is hidden, but you can find it.'
'How?' said Roland.
'Make the door appear: think it: force it with your mind. The power you know fleetingly in your world is here as real as swords. We have nothing like it. Now close your eyes. Can you still see the Mound in your thought?'

32

'Yes.'

'There is a door in the Mound,' said Malebron. 'A door.'

'What kind of door?' said Roland.

'It does not matter. Any door. The door you know best. Think of the feel of it. The sound of it. A door. The door. The only door. It must come. Make it come.'

Roland thought of the front door at home. He saw the blisters in the paint, and the brass flap with 'Letters' outlined in dry metal polish. He had been cleaning it only yesterday.

'I can see it.'

'Is it there? Is it firm? Could you touch it?' said Malebron.

'I think so,' said Roland.

'Then open your eyes. Is it still there?'

'No. It's just a hill.'

'It is still there!' said Malebron. 'It is real! You have made it with your mind! Your mind is real! You can see the door! The Mound must break! It cannot hide the door!'

'Yes,' said Roland. 'It's there. The door. It's real.'

'Then look! Now!'

Roland opened his eyes, and he saw the frame of the porch stamped in the turf, ghostly on the black hill. And as he looked the frame quivered, and without really changing, became another door; pale as moonlight, grey as ashwood; low; a square, stone arch made of three slabs – two upright and a lintel. Below it was a step carved with spiral patterns that seemed to revolve without moving. Light spread from the doorway to Roland's feet.

'The door will be open as long as you hold it in your memory,' said Malebron.

Alan Garner

Matthew, chapter 14, verses 22–33 *tells of Jesus walking on the Sea of Galilee, and of Peter's attempt to do the same. This passage (and the above excerpt from Alan Garner's novel* Elidor) *could be used in class discussion about the extent to which mind (and faith) can overcome the apparent laws of nature.*

3: THE SPIRITUAL HEALER

The editor interviewed this spiritual healer in East Anglia for a radio programme. In some ways it is as unlikely a story as the last (fictional) passage, yet this man did genuinely appear to be able to use the power of his mind to 'get things done'.

He'd attracted some attention in the local paper and I'd gone out to see him at work and to interview him for a radio programme. From the start he impressed me by insisting he wasn't a faith healer, he didn't need his 'patients' to believe in him. All he did was to hold their hands and a healing power would be channelled into them. When I watched him at work, this was all that happened. He sat facing the sick person, held their hands in his and kept silent. And the patients said it felt as though some sort of electricity was passing into them, and every time they had this treatment they got a bit better. And apparently, so far as I and a doctor could tell, quite genuine cases of arthritis and even more serious illnesses had been cured by this man.

But oddly what impressed me most was that he'd cured a horse. This horse had been lame for some time, quite badly lame, with a growth on its pastern, part of its foot. And the faith healer laid his hands on the horse's leg, and the leg had got quite hot and by next morning the horse was galloping around the field, to the amazement of its owner and the local vet.

When I took the interview I had recorded along to the studio, the engineer on duty was unimpressed.

'Do you really believe there were real cures?' he asked.

'Well, I saw it.'

'Yes, but, there must be some explanation, some rational explanation, I mean, things like that don't happen. They can't.'

Now I suspect he was just saying what many people think; that there has got to be a logical explanation for everything, and that what we think of as the natural laws of the universe can't be broken. That, if you like, there can't be such a thing as a miracle.

Maybe that's so; there is a logical explanation for such events if only we can find it.

But may there be more things in heaven and earth than are dreamed of in our philosophy? Can the mind achieve the apparently impossible by overcoming the 'laws' of nature?

Perhaps the dangerous remark is to say, 'That could never be'. By keeping an open mind, then at least there's the possibility that our lives will be enlarged to include a new mysterious, spiritual dimension.

David Self

34

4: GEORGE STEPHENSON

*George Stephenson, who played such an important part in the develop-
ment of railways, was a man close to the heart of all successful Victorians.
He was to them an outstanding example of a self-made man, rising from
poverty to affluence, through 'thrift, sobriety, and industry'. He knew
what he wanted to do, and he 'got things done'.*

George Stephenson was born on the 9th of June, 1781, in the
colliery village of Wylam, where his father was employed as a
colliery fireman. Bearing in mind the backwardness and isolation
of a mining village at that time, young Stephenson had no opportunities to avail himself of, and every possible handicap to overcome. Like other workingmen's children he was put to work at
the age of eight, and after various jobs he became at fourteen an
assistant fireman at Dewley Colliery, at the wage of a shilling a
day. He early showed an inventive mind and could turn his hand
to many things. An automatic cradle-rocker, a mechanical scare-
crow, a lamp which burnt under water (extremely useful for river
fishing, or rather poaching), an alarm clock, and glass tubes for
growing straight cucumbers are all attributed to him. His
mechanical ingenuity won him rapid promotion, so that at the
age of thirty-one he found himself comfortably off in the responsible post of engine-wright at Killingworth Colliery at a salary of
£100 a year.

*It was while he was in that job that he built his first locomotive. Some
years later he heard that a rich Darlington businessman, Edward Pease,
was considering building a horse drawn railway from Darlington to the
mouth of the river Tees.*

Stephenson visited Pease and persuaded him to substitute steam
engines for horses, and to put himself in charge of building the
railway. Stephenson already had a terrific faith in the locomotive
and pushed the idea with zeal sufficient to win the support of the
local men, who alone had the money necessary to back such a
new venture. This zeal was necessary since Stephenson had much
prejudice to overcome. Landowners feared for their fox-coverts,
the newspapers called him a 'maniac, fit only for bedlam', even
a parson denounced him from his pulpit, while Parliament was at
the best lukewarm and at one Parliamentary committee it was
insinuated that he was either insane or a foreigner.

In 1825 the next great railway was initiated, the Manchester-Liverpool line, and built by Stephenson. The engine chosen for operation on the railway was selected by open competition. The winning locomotive was the famous 'Rocket' built by Stephenson's son Robert, which achieved the remarkable speed of thirty-five miles per hour.

With the completion of the Manchester railway Stephenson's work was to a large extent completed. Within a decade Britain was in the throes of a railway boom and new financiers and new engines had come to the forefront, but the pioneer was the self-made man, George Stephenson.

David Dougan and *Frank Graham*

5: FUND-RAISING

This newspaper account describes what was achieved by one small community, and may be an incentive to 'get things done' for people not in a position to help themselves (like George Stephenson, in the previous passage).

The Norfolk village of Thurne handed over a cheque for £4000 for a kidney machine, and that, said Dr J. Pryor, of the renal unit of the Norfolk and Norwich Hospital, marked the culmination of 'a really tremendous effort'.

The population of Thurne is a mere 145, yet the bulk of the money was raised in forty weeks since Easter – an average of £100 a week.

The handing-over of the cheque took place where it all began – at the village Methodist church. It was here that the idea was mooted by a Sunday school teacher, Mr David Teager, who, with two teachers, Miss Pamela Brooks and Miss Shirley Shreeve, worked unceasingly for the cause.

'It started as a Sunday school effort, but soon the whole village responded,' said the school superintendent, Mrs Audrey Alexander. 'I think everybody in the village did something. It was hectic, but we were amazed at the result. We did not expect to do it in this time.'

The original target had been £3000 but, as costs rose, so the workers raised their sights by £1000. A sponsored walk by the children and other church members brought in £500. There was a wide range of events and donations came in from firms.

Dr Pryor said that he had been in Norfolk for five and a half years, fighting to provide a kidney service for patients. Without any effort of his own he had received a continuing flow of cheques and cash from all over the county.

Amazing amounts had been raised in small communities and the total was 'quite shattering'.

When he spoke of this at international meetings he attended, people were overwhelmed to hear that, in Britain, which had a national health service, there was still this generosity from individuals.

Eastern Counties Newspapers

5

Prison and freedom

1: BISHOP LEONARD WILSON

Not everyone who is imprisoned deserves to be. Leonard Wilson was Bishop of Singapore when it was captured by the Japanese in World War II. He was arrested and taken to Changi Jail. This account is from the diary kept by another clergyman, the Reverend John Hayter.

In the evening of his arrival Leonard was questioned, the interrogation being punctuated with beatings, for between three and four hours. On the following morning, he was again taken to the torture room, where he was made to kneel down. A three-angled bar was placed behind his knees. He was made to kneel on his haunches. His hands were tied behind his back and pulled up to a position between his shoulder blades. His head was forced down and he remained in this position for seven and a half hours. Any attempt to ease the strain from the cramp in his thighs was frustrated by the guards, who brought the flat of their hobnailed boots down hard on to his thighs. At intervals the bar between his knees would be twisted, or the guards would jump on to one or both projecting ends. Beatings and kicks were frequent. Throughout the whole of this time he was being questioned and told that he was a spy. This was one of the times when he lost his nerve and pleaded for death.

Again, the next morning, he was brought up from the cells, and this time tied face upwards to a table with his head hanging over the end of it. For several hours he remained in that position while relays of soldiers beat him systematically from the ankles to the thighs with three-fold knotted ropes.

John Hayter

38

On 13 October 1946, three years after these events, Bishop Wilson
preached at a service broadcast by the BBC:

After my first beating I was almost afraid to pray for courage lest I
should have another opportunity for exercising it, but my
unspoken prayer was there, and without God's help I doubt
whether I could have come through. Long hours of ignoble pain
were a severe test. In the middle of that torture they asked me if I
still believed in God. When, by God's help, I said, 'I do,' they
asked my why God did not save me, and by the help of his Holy
Spirit, I said, 'God does save me. He does not save me by freeing
me from pain or punishment, but he saves me by giving me the
spirit to bear it.' And when they asked me why I did not curse
them, I told them that it was because I was a follower of Jesus
Christ, who taught us that we were all brethren. I did not like to
use the words, 'Father, forgive them'. It seemed too blasphem-
ous to use Our Lord's words, but I felt them.

Leonard Wilson

2: SEVEN YEARS IN A
COMMUNIST JAIL

Dr Edith Bone suffered seven years of wrongful imprisonment in Hun-
gary. On her return to this country, she was asked how she kept her
mental balance during seven years of solitary confinement and total
isolation, six months of the time in total darkness.

There are things one must avoid and things one must do. One
must avoid being sorry for oneself and one must find things to do,
things that are a challenge to one's ingenuity. Further, it is always
good fun to get the better of one's jailors. What did I do? At first,
while I was in the dark, I made up limericks and scurrilous
doggerel poking fun at the stupid baboons who guarded me.
Then I devised a means of knowing when one of the warders was
looking in at me through the spy-hole so I could put on a little act
for their benefit when they imagined I had no notion of being
watched. I made a little abacus of breadcrumbs and straw, and
when they asked me what it was, I said as solemnly as an owl that
it was a new kind of calculating machine permitting calculations
of an intricate nature up to one million millions. Or one day I
asked for a hair-cut. The sergeant-in-charge said I was not

entitled to a hair-cut, being a woman and women being supposed to have long hair. Well, I did have long hair and as I had neither comb nor clip nor anything else to keep my hair tidy, I looked like a cave-woman, with my hair hanging into my eyes. So I tore off my hair thread by thread. It was a lengthy operation, it took me some three weeks as I had not worked out a proper technique I cut my fingers rather badly and the cuts festered. The whole thing got on the nerves of the guards, which was just what I was after. Six months later my hair had grown again and I repeated the operation, this time with a better technique. After a further six months I had just started a third 'operation haircut' when the sergeant-in-charge informed me that there was no need for it as the barber would be coming the next day to cut my hair. This was a triumph of mind over matter and gave me much pleasure. Then I began to make clocks – first a water clock and later a torsion clock, which was very accurate but had to be wound up every three minutes so that it was not really satisfactory after all.

Dr Edith Bone

3: IN PRISON IN CHILE

In 1975, a British doctor, Dr Sheila Cassidy, who was working in Chile, was imprisoned for giving medical aid to a wounded revolutionary. She gave this account of her experiences in an interview with Richard Dowden, published in the Catholic Herald *in 1976.*

I'd been working as head of the Casualty Department at Leicester Royal Infirmary for nearly three years and I found that this work, though rewarding, was leading to more and more administration. I decided I wanted a break to see another part of the world.

I had some Chilean friends who told me how beautiful Chile was, so in December, 1971, I went there, originally just for six months. When I got there I found I loved the country. Its people and their way of life appealed to me enormously, so I started to learn Spanish and to study for the Chilean medical degree.

When I returned to Chile in February, 1975, I worked in a government emergency hospital. . . .

My arrest was as a result of an incident which began when the hiding place of the three chief members of the revolutionary left-wing movement, MIR, was discovered. There was a big gun-battle and one man was killed. The other two got away with their wives and a nine-month old baby.

Nelson Gutierez, the second in command of the MIR, received two bullet wounds in his leg. After being on the run for nearly a week he got to one of the Church offices in Santiago. No one knows how. When the priests arrived for work in the morning, they found him there.

The priests decided to help Nelson Gutierez not for political reasons but because they saw it as their Christian duty. They arranged for him to be looked after in the house of the Sisters of Notre Dame and they then approached me and asked me if I would treat him.

He had no other chance of medical treatment, so I had no hesitation in seeing him. I visited him twice in the course of a week and on the second visit his condition was so bad – he had a fever and impending septicaemia – that I advised the priests that he needed hospital treatment and should seek political asylum.

I don't know how the information that I treated him leaked out, but they arrested me at the house of the Columban Fathers where I was visiting a convalescing nun. They attacked it with machine guns and killed one of the maids there.

I was taken by the secret police, the DINA, to a torture house where I was stripped naked and tortured with electrodes strapped to my body. . . .

I was in prison with about 120 other women and about 500 men. I spent three weeks in the solitary confinement area where there were about twenty to thirty other people in the cells. In the house of torture there must have been about thirty other people. . . .

Prayer kept me going in prison even when I thought they were going to kill me. It has always been very important to me, especially in these last eighteen months. During this time I have been going to Mass daily and praying in a disciplined way.

While I was in prison I fought continually with the commandant to try to get him to allow us to have Mass daily. He kept promising us, but during the five weeks I was there we were only allowed to hear Mass on Christmas Eve.

Every Sunday, at the request of the other prisoners, I held a brief liturgy. We read psalms and passages from the New Testament and we broke bread in a symbolic manner. The second Sunday I did this fifty people came and prayed with me.

Dr Sheila Cassidy

4: PRISONERS OF CONSCIENCE

This passage is part of a statement to the press, issued by Cardinal Basil Hume, Archbishop of Westminster, in 1977 (which was Prisoner of Conscience Year).

Sender Levinzon from Bendery in the USSR is twenty-nine years of age. About two years ago he was sentenced to six years in a strict regime labour camp. His wife and two young children are already in Israel. It seems that the 'crime' for which he has been sentenced is his strenuous campaign to emigrate to Israel with his family.

Then there is Petras Plumpa, a Lithuanian and a Roman Catholic layman. He is in his late thirties and was sentenced in 1973 for publishing the truth as he saw it about his Church and in defence of religious freedom. He was sentenced to eight years in a strict regime camp.

Then there are two prisoners from Latin America. Guillermo Beausire Alonso has a British father and a British passport. In November 1974, he was arrested in Buenos Aires by officials of DINA (the Chilean National Directorate of Intelligence) and taken back to Santiago. With other members of his family, he was held as hostage for Andres Pascal Allende, an important leader of the MIR (Movement of the Revolutionary Left). The others were released, but Guillermo Beausire Alonso has, since that time, been held in a number of detention centres, but never moved to an official prison. The Chilean authorities have consistently refused to acknowledge that he is in detention. He was last seen in May 1975, when he appeared to be very ill and had lost about two stone in weight.

Toroteo Grandel is a Paraguayan peasant farmer, a middle-aged man with a family. He was arrested on 21 May 1976 at his home in Tobarti by soldiers of the second infantry division of the army. He was subsequently detained in Gaaguazu military camp. This was only a few days after he had travelled to Asuncion, Paraguay's capital, to testify about the burning of homes and maltreatment of peasant families by the military in the district of Yhu where his village is situated. He is still in detention although the authorities deny this. He was last seen at the military barracks of the second infantry division in Villarica in December 1976.

In Latin America there is evidence of increasing brutality by security forces. The use of psychological torture and physical pain by cigarette ends, electrodes, by tearing off finger nails, has become more common in countries like Chile, Uruguay and Argentina. Again, throughout the Soviet Union and elsewhere in the Soviet bloc, men and women are, to the best of my information, being imprisoned and tortured solely for the views they conscientiously hold.

Cardinal Basil Hume

Amnesty International

is an international human rights organization which campaigns for the release of Prisoners of Conscience, provided they have not used or advocated violence, throughout the world, from Argentina to the USSR., from South Africa to Ethiopia. 116 countries are listed in Amnesty International's last Annual Report. Amnesty International's estimate of prisoners of conscience detained at any one time is 500,000. Much of the pressure for their release came from Amnesty International with its thirty-seven National Sections and members in seventy countries, and 2000 groups throughout the world.

For information about Amnesty's work, write to Amnesty International, British Section, Tower House, 8–14 Southampton Street, London WC2E 7HF.

5: FREEDOM TO BREATHE

In 1945, Alexander Solzhenitsyn was imprisoned for remarks he had made about Stalin. For the next eight years he was in labour camps, including a 'special' camp for long term prisoners.

He has written many books and now lives in the West. In this short 'prose poem' he writes about the joy of freedom so many of us take for granted.

A shower fell in the night and now dark clouds drift across the sky, occasionally sprinkling a fine film of rain.

I stand under an apple tree in blossom and I breathe. Not only the apple tree but the grass round it glistens with moisture; words cannot describe the sweet fragrance that pervades the air. Inhaling as deeply as I can, the aroma invades my whole being; I breathe with my eyes open, I breathe with my eyes closed – I cannot say which gives me the greater pleasure.

This, I believe, is the single most precious freedom that prison takes away from us; the freedom to breathe freely, as I now can. No food on earth, no wine, not even a woman's kiss is sweeter to me than this air steeped in the fragrance of flowers, of moisture and freshness.

No matter that this is only a tiny garden, hemmed in by five-storey houses like cages in a zoo. I cease to hear the motorcycles backfiring, the radios whining, the burble of loud-speakers. As long as there is fresh air to breathe under an apple tree after a shower, we may survive a little longer.

Alexander Solzhenitsyn

Psalm 142 is said to be a psalm of David, a prayer composed when he was imprisoned in a cave.

6
Famous Christians

1: MOTHER TERESA

A woman lay dying on a Calcutta pavement. Her feet were half
eaten away by rats and ants. She had been lying there for days
and no one had taken any notice of her.

Then a nun came along. She was a tiny woman, dressed in a
white sari which hung loosely about her and covered her head.
She walked quickly, for she was always in a hurry. Her name was
Mother Teresa.

When she saw the woman on the pavement she stopped. Full
of pity, she picked her up and carried her into a nearby hospital
for treatment. They told her there that the woman was too ill and
poor to bother about. Besides, they had no room. Mother Teresa
pleaded with them, but they said there was nothing they could
do for her. However, she would not leave her patient, and set off
for another hospital. But it was in vain. The woman died.

For five years Mother Teresa and her helpers tended the sick
and dying on the streets. The hospitals were full and there was
nowhere else to take them. They even had to beg for medicines to
treat their patients.

But Mother Teresa knew the situation could not continue.

She took her problem to the city council of Calcutta. She begged
the council to give her a place where people could die with
someone to love and care for them. 'It is a shame for people to die
on our city roads,' she said.

The health officer showed her a building near the great Hindu
temple, Kalighat. He suggested she might use part of it for her
purpose. It was once used as a rest-house where Hindus came

after they had worshipped their goddess. Now it was used by thugs and layabouts as a place for gambling and drinking.

Mother Teresa knew that most of the city's poor came here to die, as it was a holy place for Hindus. It did not matter to her whether her patients were Hindus, Buddhists, Sikhs or Muslims. She just wanted to show these poor, sick people the love of Jesus. As the Bible says, 'When you do it to these my brothers you do it to me.' She gladly accepted the building and within twenty-four hours she brought her first patients here.

Mother Teresa and her Sisters have taken in over 36,000 people off the streets. Half of them die quite soon afterwards, but Mother Teresa is content that they die peacefully. 'They understand that even if they have only a few hours left to live, they are loved. However dirty and sick they are, someone cares for them.'

Audrey Constant

2: WILLIAM BOOTH

The Salvation Army was founded in 1865 by William Booth. But that was not its name at first – it used to be called the East London Christian Mission.

William Booth was brought up in Nottingham. When he lost his job he moved to London to find new work. In his spare time he went around preaching, either in churches or on street corners, or anywhere else where people would listen.

After his marriage he was for a few years a Church minister. He preached in churches up and down the country. But this was not what he felt God wanted him to do. He believed God wished him to reach the ordinary people of the land, and therefore he had to take his message to the people in the streets. With his wife Catherine and their children, he returned to London. There were thousands of people in the capital who needed to hear God's word.

One day Booth was asked to preach at an open-air meeting in the East End of London. It was outside the Blind Beggar public house in Whitechapel. A crowd came to listen. They laughed at him and threw bad eggs, but he did not care. When he got home that night he knew what his future was to be.

'I have found my destiny,' he told his wife. 'I must take the Gospel to the people of the East End.'

A few days later he was asked to preach at some meetings in the East End. They were to be held in a large tent on an open space known as Mile End Waste. Booth agreed – this was just the opportunity he wanted.

The meetings in the tent were noisy, with drunks and trouble-makers causing an uproar. Once, the ropes holding up the tent were cut, bringing the tent down on the crowd inside. Another time, winds ripped the canvas, leaving gaping holes that let in the rain.

As the weather became colder, Booth stopped using the tent. For some weeks he rented the East London Theatre. Sometimes he used a dance hall for his meetings, and he even preached in a hayloft.

One of his converts was Peter Monk, a famous Irish boxer. He became Booth's bodyguard. If there was any sign of trouble at a meeting, Monk took off his coat and rolled up his sleeves. While Booth preached, the boxer kept order!

Geoffrey Hanks

The title 'Christian Mission' was soon dropped, and the organization was named the Salvation Army. William Booth was its General.

3: ELIZABETH FRY

Elizabeth Fry (1780–1845) was a Quaker who became famous for her work as a prison reformer. Before her marriage, she was called Elizabeth Gurney; the family were all Quakers, living in Norwich. Elizabeth had six sisters and four brothers.

Unusually for that time, the family did not live the life of 'Plain Quakers', wearing dark, plain clothes and believing music and dancing were wicked. They lived in high society, and Elizabeth was not too fond of attending the Quaker Meeting House.

This story has been arranged for five readers, though it could be adapted to be read by one or two voices.

Narrator: One Sunday in February 1798, there came to preach in Norwich an American Quaker, William Savery.

Elizabeth (*sulky*): I agreed to go to the Meeting House although I had a very bad pain in my stomach.

Narrator: Savery preached a sermon. Elizabeth was much impressed; and cried all the way home.

Elizabeth (*sobbing*): . . . Owing to having heard much excellence from one who appears to me a true Christian I have today felt there is a God. . . .

Narrator: It was perhaps from this moment that Elizabeth Gurney's faith began to grow. By the year 1800, she had met another man who was to influence her, another Quaker, Joseph Fry. In August of that year, they married.

Elizabeth: . . . In the presence of the Lord and of this assembly I take this, my Friend Joseph Fry to be my husband, promising by Divine assistance to be unto him a loving and faithful wife, until it shall please the Lord by death to separate us.

Narrator: Elizabeth and Joseph moved from Norwich to London. In the next twenty-two years, they had eleven children. Elizabeth Fry, who now wore the plain, dark dresses and white head-dress worn by most Quaker women, also found time to preach at many Quaker meeting houses. Then in 1813 she heard about the conditions of Newgate Prison. The person who stirred her conscience was a French Quaker, Stephen Grellet, who had visited the prison.

Grellet: I was astonished beyond description at the woe and misery I beheld. I found many prisoners very sick, lying on the bare floor or on some old straw, having very scanty clothing, though it was quite cold. There were several young children there, almost naked. They had been born in prison. They have never had clothes.

Narrator: Elizabeth immediately gathered together a number of women Friends and organized a huge sewing party, making clothes for the prisoners. Next day, with one companion, she went to the prison and asked the governor to grant her permission to visit the women prisoners.

Governor: I do not think it would be right. The convicts, they are . . . well, I do not like visiting them myself.

Elizabeth: Tush! Now do thou stand aside!

Governor: Madam, pray at least leave your watch for safe keeping – the pickpockets would you know . . .

Narrator: Elizabeth and her friend were admitted to the prison.

Elizabeth (*remembering that day*): There were three hundred women in two rooms. Some had been sentenced to death. Others were waiting for trial. More than anything, I was moved to see two prisoners tearing the clothes from a baby that had died to clothe one still alive.

Narrator: Next day Elizabeth returned with clean straw for the sick and more clothes for the prison children. Over the years, her work continued.

Elizabeth: I am much occupied in forming a school in Newgate for the younger children of prisoners, as well as for the younger criminals.

Narrator: She had trouble persuading the authorities.

Governor: It is an admirable plan. It does you credit, Mistress Fry. But you do not understand the problem. Even the children are vicious. And anyway there is no suitable room.

Elizabeth: Is it only lack of space that prevents the experiment?

Narrator: She found a room in the prison, and the experiment went ahead. The Governor and his committee were forced to report the success of Elizabeth Fry's work.

Governor: The benevolent work of Mistress Fry and her friends in the female department of the prison has indeed, by the establishment of a school, by providing work and encouraging industrious habits, produced the most gratifying change.

Narrator: Elizabeth Fry became a public figure, known throughout the country. And everywhere she went she preached; for example, in Bridewell Prison in Glasgow. A woman who was present there wrote an account of the visit.

Scotswoman: Mistress Fry took off her bonnet and sat on a low seat facing one hundred women prisoners. She took the Bible and read the parables of the lost sheep and of the prodigal son. . . . She often paused and looked at the women with tenderness and quickly won their confidence. The reading was followed by a solemn pause, and then, resting her Bible on the ground, there was Mistress Fry kneeling before the women. Her prayer was beyond words.

Narrator: Elizabeth Fry brought old clothing and other comforts to the prisoners. She persuaded them to follow new rules of behaviour, and in return the authorities promised to improve the conditions of the prison. But her work was not approved of by everyone. Her beliefs were mocked in the House of Commons, and prison inspectors reintroduced severe punishments. Even so she continued to devote her life to prison reform, driven by her concern for her fellow-beings and determined to put her beliefs into action.

Elizabeth: I desire to do justly, love mercy and walk humbly with my God.

David Self

4: DIETRICH BONHOEFFER

Bonhoeffer (1906–45) was a pastor or minister in the German Lutheran church who became famous for his writings and teachings and especially for his resistance against Nazism. His life raises the debating point: Is assassination (or other revolutionary acts) ever justified?

In about 1932 Bonhoeffer underwent a profound experience and this converted him from being a formal Christian into a totally committed one. Although fundamentally uninterested in politics, Bonhoeffer was horrified by the Nazis' accession to power in 1933 and particularly by their anti-semitism. As a young pastor in Berlin he appealed to his fellow clergy to go on strike; they should refuse to conduct funerals until the Nazis moderated their policies. This came to nothing but Bonhoeffer became a leading figure in the movement that denounced Nazi interference into the affairs of the church.

Bonhoeffer served for a while as pastor to a Lutheran church in London and then returned to Germany to run a seminary for student clergymen. In 1939 he went on a lecture tour to the United States and could easily have remained there. However, with war imminent he felt that his place was back in Germany – he had to go 'back to the trenches' as he put it.

In the final phase of his life, Bonhoeffer threw himself into the underground resistance movement against Hitler. Acute moral dilemmas might seem to be involved. The Lutheran faith, to which Bonhoeffer belonged, lays special stress upon faithful citizenship being a primary Christian duty. Yet here he was committing high treason in war time.

The only sure way to get rid of Hitler was to assassinate him: this could be construed as murder. Being involved in the resistance meant a life of constant lying and deception. Bonhoeffer showed no sign of being in a moral dilemma – he believed that Jesus was impelling him. However, he did realize that he might tarnish his public reputation so much that he would be unable to continue as a pastor.

Bonhoeffer was arrested in 1943. The extent of the conspiracy and of Bonhoeffer's involvement was not realized by the Nazi authorities, but at Easter 1945 Bonhoeffer was moved to Flossenburg concentration camp, and there, within sound of the American guns, they stripped him naked; he knelt in prayer and then they hanged him.

Colin Cross

5: ST FRANCIS OF ASSISI

St Francis, the founder of the Order of the Franciscans, was born in either 1181 or 1182. The son of a rich merchant, he became disenchanted with worldly wealth and, after being disowned by his father, he devoted himself to repairing a ruined church.

One day, in 1208, he was in church and heard read aloud Christ's command to his disciples that they should leave everything and follow him. Francis took this as an instruction to himself and gathered together a band of followers. Out of this grew the Franciscan Order of Friars and its sister order of nuns, the Clares.

Francis became famous for the simplicity of his life, his generosity, his love of nature and his humility.

In 1224, he received the Stigmata (see below); and died in 1226.

Two years after his death, a man called Thomas of Celano wrote the first biography of Francis. These are two short extracts:

(a) Receiving of the Stigmata

Whilst he was staying in the hermitage which is called Alverna after the place where it is situated, two years before he gave his soul back to heaven, he saw in a vision from God a man like a seraph having six wings standing above him, with hands extended and feet together, fixed on to a cross. Two wings were raised above his head, two were outstretched for flight, and two covered his whole body. And when the blessed servant of the Most High saw this, he was filled with exceedingly great wonder but he did not know what this vision signified.

He also experienced intense feelings of joy and gladness in the kindly and gracious expression with which the seraph (whose beauty was indeed beyond all description) looked at him; yet he was completely overwhelmed with fear at the crucifixion and the harshness of the seraph's sufferings. Thus he arose, sorrowful and rejoicing, so to speak, and joy and grief alternated in him. He anxiously considered what this vision indicated, and in anguish he struggled to reach understanding. And while he could still not clearly perceive anything, and the strangeness of this vision was claiming his entire attention, in his hands and his feet there began to appear the marks of nails, such as he had just seen in the crucified man who had stood above him.

His hands and feet seemed to be pierced in the middle by nails, the heads of the nails being visible in the inner side of the hands and the upper side of the feet, and the points of the nails on the other side. For those marks were round on the inner side of the hands, and oblong on the outer side, and certain small pieces of flesh were seen projecting from the rest of the flesh, like the ends of nails bent and driven back. In the same way the marks of nails were impressed in his feet and raised above the rest of the flesh. His right side also was covered by a scar as if it had been pierced with a lance, and often it discharged blood, so that his tunic and breeches were many times sprinkled with the holy blood. Alas, how few people, while the crucified servant of the crucified Lord was alive, were thought worthy to see the sacred wound in his side!

(b) Love of animals

For when one day he had arrived at the castle called Alviano in order to preach the word of God, he went up on to a high point so that all the people could see him, and began to ask for silence. All the people were quiet and respectfully stood waiting, but there were a large number of swallows building nests in the same place, and they were chirping and chattering loudly. Because their chirping effectively prevented anyone from hearing him, blessed Francis spoke to the birds and said: 'My sisters the swallows, now it is time for me to speak also, because you have said enough up till now. Listen to the word of God, and hold yourselves in silence and quiet until the sermon of the Lord is finished.' And those little birds, much to the amazement of all those present, at once became silent, nor did they move from that place until the preaching was ended. Those men, when they had seen this sign, were filled with the greatest sense of wonder and said, 'Here indeed is a holy man, a friend of the Most High.' And they hurried with the greatest devotion to touch at least his clothes, praising and blessing God.

Matthew, chapter 10, verses 7–19 *is the passage that inspired Francis to start his order. See also page 215.*

7
War and peace

1: THE BULLDOG

The horrors of war are often most clearly illustrated by the comparatively small incident. This story comes from a book called The Hiding Place. *The story-teller is Corrie ten Boom who became a heroine of the anti-Nazi underground movement in Holland in the early years of World War II. She was about fifty at this time and lived with her sister and their old father who was a watch-maker.*

At this time, the Nazis made all Jews wear a yellow star – including a man Corrie had nicknamed the Bulldog.

This was not only because we never saw him without two large bulldogs on the end of a leash but because, with his wrinkled, jowly face and short bowlegs he looked exactly like one of his own pets. His obvious affection for the animals was what touched us; as they went along he constantly muttered and fussed at them. Father and the Bulldog always tipped their hats to one another ceremoniously as we passed.

One day, Father and I, on our usual walk, saw something so very unusual that we both stopped in mid-stride. Walking toward us along the sidewalk, as so many hundreds of times before, came the Bulldog with his rolling short-legged gait. The bright yellow star had by now ceased to look extraordinary, so what – and then I knew what was wrong. The dogs. The dogs were not with him!

'Permit an introduction, Sir,' Father began. 'I am Casper ten Boom and this is my daughter, Cornelia.'

The Bulldog shook hands and again I noticed the deep creases in the sagging cheeks. 'Harry de Vries,' he said.

'Mr de Vries, we've so often admired your – er – affection for your bulldogs. We hope they are well?'

The squat little man stared from one of us to the other. Slowly the heavy-rimmed eyes filled with tears. 'Are they well?' he repeated. 'I believe they are well. I hope that they are well. They are dead.'

'Dead!' we said together.

'I put the medicine in their bowl with my own hand and I petted them to sleep. My little ones. If you could have seen them eat! I waited, you know, till we had enough coupons for meat. They used to have meat all the time.'

We stared at him dumbly. 'Was it,' I ventured at last, 'was it because of the rationing?'

'Miss ten Boom, I am a Jew. Who knows when they will come to take me away?'

Corrie ten Boom

2: BELSEN

Just how inhuman man can be to his fellow man was revealed when allied troops first entered the Nazi concentration camps at the end of World War II. This was a BBC report from one of the camps, Belsen.

I picked my way over corpse after corpse in the gloom until I heard one voice raised above the gentle undulating moaning. I found a girl, she was a living skeleton, impossible to gauge her age for she had practically no hair left, and her face was only a yellow parchment sheet with two holes in it for eyes. She was stretching out her stick of an arm and gasping something, it was 'English, English, medicine, medicine', and she was trying to cry but she hadn't enough strength. And beyond her down the passage and in the hut there were the convulsive movements of dying people too weak to raise themselves from the floor.

In the shade of some trees lay a great collection of bodies. I walked about them trying to count, there were perhaps 150 of them flung down on eath other, all naked, all so thin that their yellow skin glistened like stretched rubber on their bones.

At one end of the pile a cluster of men and women were gathered round a fire; they were using rags and old shoes taken from the bodies to keep it alight, and they were heating soup over it. And close by was the enclosure where 500 children between the ages of five and twelve had been kept. They were not so hungry as the rest, for the women had sacrificed themselves to keep them alive. Babies were born at Belsen, some of them shrunken, wizened little things that could not live, because their mothers could not feed them.

One woman, distraught to the point of madness, flung herself at a British soldier who was on guard at the camp on the night that it was reached by the Eleventh Armoured Division; she begged him to give her some milk for the tiny baby she held in her arms. She laid the mite on the ground and threw herself at the sentry's feet and kissed his boots. And when, in his distress, he asked her to get up, she put the baby in his arms and ran off crying that she would find milk for it because there was no milk in her breast. And when the soldier opened the bundle of rags to look at the child, he found that it had been dead for days.

Richard Dimbleby

3: FIRESTORM

There are two ways in which fires can originate in a nuclear explosion. First, by the ignition of trash, window curtains, rugs, bedspreads, leaves, dry grass and similar combustible material, as a result of the heat radiated by the explosion. Second, by upset stoves, electrical short circuits, and broken gas lines caused by the blast. The heat from a twenty-megaton air burst would be intense enough to start many fires at eighteen miles from the point of detonation.

To compound the danger of thousands of uncontrolled individual fires, a phenomenon known as a firestorm is likely to develop when a large area is burning. As the superheated air from the fires rises, it creates a huge vacuum, into which rushes a mass of fresh air, in much the same way that a chimney draught operates. At times, especially at the edges of the fire, this fresh air may move in at hurricane speeds.

Following the atomic bombing of Hiroshima, the firestorm developed after twenty minutes, achieved its maximum intensity after about two hours, and subsided after six hours, by which time it had burned out an area of four and a half square miles.

Tom Stonier

The scene was described by the head of the Internal Medicine Department of the Communications Hospital.

Between the Red Cross Hospital and the centre of the city I saw nothing that wasn't burned to a crisp. Streetcars were standing at Kawaya-cho and Kamiya-cho and inside were dozens of bodies, blackened beyond recognition. I saw fire reservoirs filled to the brim with dead people who looked as though they had been boiled alive. In one reservoir I saw a man, horribly burned, crouching beside another man who was dead. He was drinking bloodstained water out of the reservoir. Even if I had tried to stop him, it wouldn't have done any good: he was completely out of his head. In one reservoir there were so many dead people there wasn't enough room for them to fall over. They must have died sitting in the water.

Even the swimming pool at the Prefectural Middle School was filled with dead people. They must have suffocated while they sat in the water trying to escape the fire because they didn't appear to be burned. . . .

That pool wasn't big enough to accommodate everybody who tried to get in. You could tell that by looking around the sides. I don't know how many were caught by death with their heads hanging over the edge. In one pool I saw some people who were still alive, sitting in the water with dead all around them. They were too weak to get out. People were trying to help them, but I am sure they must have died. . . .

Dr Hanaoka

4: SACRIFICE OF AN ISLAND

In wartime, many people lose their homes. Some people lose them in peacetime as well. In 1946, the United States government decided to use the island of Bikini, an atoll in the South Pacific for atom-bomb tests.

Early in 1946, an American naval officer – a man gifted with a flowery and persuasive turn of phrase – stepped ashore at Bikini and, without ceremony, informed the islanders that the war was over and they had an opportunity to make a sacrifice in the interests of world peace. He likened them to the Children of Israel – a comparison which has not been forgotten over the years, as they have wandered from island to island, waiting for a permanent resting-place.

The 'sacrifice' he talked about was that they should leave Bikini and let the Americans use the area to test atomic weapons. At the time, they expected to return in about two years – having made their contribution to international stability.

As it turned out, the tests went on for twelve years – twenty-three tests in all, including an H-bomb explosion that went disastrously wrong. The cloud from the bomb floated away from the area, smothering nearby islands – and a passing Japanese fishing boat – with radioactive particles. Many islanders, some of the fishermen and a number of American servicemen later manifested the symptoms of radiation poisoning – developing cancer of one form or another.

Eventually, the tests were abandoned and, in the late Sixties, the American government pronounced Bikini safe for the islanders to return to.

It had changed somewhat: soil thought to contain radioactive substances had been bulldozed away, vegetation had been cleared and 50,000 coconut palms had been imported from areas which had not had the nuclear experience. Concrete houses replaced the traditional thatched huts of the area.

The Bikini islanders settled down to something like their old existence. They took back their land, grew vegetables and fished again in the well-stocked lagoon.

But the scientists had, apparently, been too hasty. In 1978, using new and more sophisticated detection equipment, they found the island was still seriously contaminated. The coconuts, the water, even the shellfish from the lagoon, were all dangerous, if consumed in large quantities.

The Bikini islanders were told they would have to leave home again – and this time for at least thirty years.

Bob Friend

In some cases, it may be relevant to link this passage with discussions on stewardship and ecology.

5: THE WORLD DISARMAMENT CAMPAIGN

This is part of an open letter written in 1981 by the Secretary of the Methodist Conference, Dr Kenneth Greet.

The five nuclear powers (USA, USSR, France, UK and China) already possess enough weapons totally to destroy recognizable life on this planet fifty times over. But every day more weapons are added to the armoury. 'The arms race' is no empty phrase. The expenditure on arms has reached astronomical proportions and it continues to escalate. The world spends about thirty million pounds an hour on military forces and weapons. Some thirty-six million men are today under arms with a further twenty-five million in reserve. About half the world's scientists and engineers are engaged on military research and development.

It is an appalling fact that high military expenditure is spreading rapidly to the developing countries. These poor parts of the world spend five times as much on arms as on agricultural machinery. It has been stated that they have one soldier for every 250 inhabitants but only one doctor for every 3700. The cost of one jet fighter could build 40,000 village pharmacies. More than twelve million children die each year of hunger before their fifth birthday. Killer diseases such as malaria, typhoid and sleeping sickness could be eradicated from the face of the globe for half the amount spent in one year on military measures. And these weapons do not keep the peace. In the Developing World since 1945 twenty million people have died in more than a hundred wars. The weapons for the slaughter of the poor are manufactured in the factories of the rich – including Britain.

With new technical innovations the old notion of 'not being the first to attack' becomes obsolete. Enhanced accuracy of aim means that under threat of war a nuclear power would seek to destroy the enemy's weapons before they could be used.

The knowledge of how to make nuclear weapons and even the resources to do so are now widely available. So the danger of proliferation is therefore acute (a number of nations did not sign the Non-Proliferation Treaty of 1970). There is also the peril of nuclear 'accident'. Nuclear deterrence is high-wire deterrence and immensely risky.

In the face of this situation men and women react in various ways. Some are very fearful and their fear is fed by television programmes and newspaper articles which assume that a nuclear holocaust is inevitable. Others close their minds to the whole appalling business. If challenged, they say, 'Why should I worry; there's nothing I can do about it anyhow.' It is true that there is not much that the individual can do. But that is no reason for yielding to the devilish temptation to do nothing at all. If we can only do a little, let us do that little as well as we can: that is the Christian response. Moreover, by combining our efforts much can be achieved.

That is why I believe the time has come for ordinary people all over the world to express their concern. Governments must be made to feel the pressure of a global revolt against the steady erosion of our security. It was President Eisenhower who said, 'Some day the demand for disarmament by hundreds of millions will, I hope, become so universal and so insistent that no man, no nation, can withstand it.'

Dr Kenneth Greet

The World Disarmament Campaign is not an appeal for unilateral disarmament but an organized way of making one's voice heard – in both the East and West. Its address is 21 Little Russell Street, London WC1A 2HN.

8
Unselfishness

1: THE FIVE LOAVES

Many people see things entirely from a selfish viewpoint. Karel Čapek, a Czech writer, imagined the reactions of a baker, living in the time of Jesus, after Jesus had performed the miracle of feeding the 5000.

The miracle is described in Mark's gospel, chapter 6, verses 30–44; Matthew's gospel, chapter 14, verses 15–33; Luke's gospel, chapter 9, verses 10–17; *and* John's gospel, chapter 6, verses 5–14.

You know, neighbour, no baker can put up with that; how could he? If it became the custom for anyone who liked to feed five thousand people with five loaves and two small fishes what would become of the bakers, tell me that? It doesn't matter so much about the fishes; they grow themselves in the water and anyone who likes can catch them. But a baker must buy flour and firewood at a high price, he must employ an assistant and pay him wages; he must keep a shop, he must pay taxes, and this, and that, and by the time he's finished he's glad if he has a few ha'pence left over for himself so that he needn't go begging. And he – he just looks up to heaven and has enough bread for five or I don't know how many thousand people; the flour doesn't cost him anything, he doesn't have to have wood carried long distances, no expenses, no work – well, of course he can give the people bread for nothing!

And he never thinks how he's depriving the bakers in the neighbourhood of their hard-earned profits! I tell you it's unfair competition and he ought to be prevented from doing it.

Karel Čapek

2: TOGETHER IN CALCUTTA AND CHITTAGONG

In response to an invitation made by some young Asians, a number of young people went from different continents to spend a few weeks living with them in Calcutta (India) and Chittagong (Bangla Desh).

Both in Calcutta and in Chittagong, their home was in very poor neighbourhoods.

Every morning they went out to work in company with many others, in the homes for the dying or for abandoned children, or in the city's slums. The afternoons were devoted to reflection about a letter to all the 'People of God' that they were going to write after their visit.

This is part of that letter.

From Calcutta and Chittagong, 1 December 1976.

Whether you be young or old, begin at once to make your own life a parable of sharing, by accomplishing concrete acts whatever the cost.

In transforming your life, nobody is asking you to opt for stark austerity without any beauty or joy.

Share everything you have, and freedom will be yours.

Resist the urge to consume – the more you buy the more you need. The accumulation of reserves, for yourself or for your children, is the beginning of injustice.

Sharing supposes a relationship of equals; it never makes others dependent. This is true both between individuals and between nations.

Sharing is also going to mean changes in where you live.

Turn your home into a place of constant welcome, a house of peace and forgiveness.

Simplify where you live, but without demanding the same of older people whose homes are filled with memories. With great age intuitions of God arise, which help the young to advance.

You have neighbours, on your staircase, or down the street. Take the time to get involved with them. You will find great loneliness. You will also see that the boundary of injustice is not only between one continent and another, but lies a few hundred yards from your door.

Invite people to share a meal. A spirit of festival has more to do with simplicity than with large quantities of food.

As a concrete expression of solidarity, certain people will go so far as to move into another neighbourhood, anxious to live among people whom society has forgotten about – the old, foreigners, immigrants. Remember that in all the world's great cities, to a greater or lesser extent, zones of poverty exist alongside zones bursting with affluence!

The parable of sharing also concerns your working life.

Spare no effort to obtain a greater equality of wages, as well as working conditions fit for human beings.

When career or competition, the desire for a high salary or consumer-demands are your basic reasons for working, you are not far from exploiting other people, or being exploited yourself.

Work to earn what you need, never to accumulate more.

Taizé Community

3: MY BROTHER'S KEEPER

The man sitting opposite me on the tube was slumped forward, his head in his hands. He groaned loudly and his body lurched from side to side with the movement of the train. I tried to pretend he wasn't there and hid behind my newspaper. I lowered my paper and looked helplessly around the carriage. It was ten in the morning and the only other occupants were two girls. They weren't together. Both of them were apparently lost in the racing edition of the Standard. One girl looked up, our eyes met and she hastily looked down again. No help there. The man continued to moan and nobody else got in the carriage and took the weight off my shoulders. Next stop Oxford Circus. Thank God, I thought, feeling in my pocket for my ticket. The train stopped. I got up. The man opposite lifted his head and looked at me. His face was covered in blood. My knees and hands were shaking. The doors opened and I got out. On the platform I turned and faced the train. The man had his head in his hands again. The girls were still intent on their papers. My feet wouldn't move, either to get back in the carriage or walk away. Then the doors closed and the train moved and the man disappeared from my sight forever. I felt guilty all day. I still do, thinking about it. Why didn't I do anything? Or the other girls for that matter. I was twenty-two, they were both younger, but we were already victims of that dreadful thing called 'not getting involved' or, as my

Grandma used to put it, 'Never trouble trouble till trouble troubles you.'

I think Louis MacNeice put it best of all, in a poem called *Bar-room Matins*:

> . . . Am I
> My brother's keeper? Let him die.
> Let him die, his death shall be
> A drop of water in the sea,
> A journalist's commodity.

Lesley Davies

Genesis, chapter 4 *(the story of Cain and Abel) is where the question 'Am I my brother's keeper?' is first posed.*

Matthew, chapter 18, verses 15–22 *is where Jesus teaches about the need to forgive (and to be responsible for) one's brother – or neighbour.*

4: SORRY!

One form of unselfishness or generosity is being able to admit you were (or still are) in the wrong. But being able to say 'sorry!' is not always all that easy. The scene of this conversation is a school corridor or playground.

Older girl: You still not speaking to that Jeremy Watkins?
Younger girl: What do you think?
Older girl: I think you ought to.
Younger girl: Oh yes? And I know what he'd say if I did. After what I called him.
Older girl: His brother told my brother he really fancies you.
Younger girl (*thinking he's after sex*):
  Ohh, that!
Older girl: No, not like that. He likes you. He wants you to say something, speak to him again. You like him, don't you? (*pause*)
Younger girl: Well, he can make the first move.
Older girl: After you said that if he ever spoke to you again, you'd get your dad to complain to his dad?
  (*slight pause*)

Younger girl: I'd like to see him again.
Older girl: Well, who's going to make the first move, then?

David Self

5: CHOPSTICKS

In Korea there is a legend about a native warrior who died and went to heaven. 'Before I enter,' he said to the gatekeeper, 'I would like you to take me on a tour of hell.' The gatekeeper found a guide to take the warrior to hell. When he got there he was astonished to see a great table piled high with the choicest foods. But the people in hell were starving.

The warrior turned to his guide and raised his eyebrows.

'It's this way,' the guide explained. 'Everybody who comes down here is given a pair of chopsticks five feet long, and is required to hold them at the end to eat. But you just can't eat with chopsticks five feet long if you hold them at the end. Look at them. They miss their mouths every time, see?'

The visitor agreed that this was hell indeed and asked to be taken back to heaven post-haste. In heaven, to his surprise, he saw a similar room, with a similar table laden with very choice foods. But the people were happy: they looked radiantly happy.

The visitor turned to the guide. 'No chopsticks, I suppose?' he said.

'Oh yes,' said the guide, 'they have the same chopsticks, the same length, and they must be held at the end just as in hell. But you see, these people have learned that if a man feeds his neighbour, his neighbour will feed him also.'

John P. Hogan

See Luke, chapter 10, verses 30–7. *The parable of the Good Samaritan is the answer Jesus gave to the question put to him by a lawyer, 'Who is my neighbour?'*

9
Looking ahead

1: THE SECRET OF THE MACHINES

We live in a world in which we are served by machinery, by silicon chips, by micro-processors – and by robots. The future will inevitably see an increase in the number and variety of robots that will be at our command – some of them possibly highly sophisticated ones, like those manufactured by Rossum.

In ten years Rossum's Universal Robots will produce so much corn, so much cloth, so much everything, that things will be practically without price. Every one will take as much as he wants. There'll be no poverty. Yes, there'll be unemployed. But, then, there won't be any employment. Everything will be done by living machines. The Robots will clothe and feed us. The Robots will make bricks and build houses for us. The Robots will keep our accounts and sweep our stairs. There'll be no employment, but everybody will be free from worry, and liberated from the degradation of labour. Everybody will live only to perfect himself. The Robots will wash the feet of the beggar and prepare a bed for him in his own house. Nobody will get bread at the price of life and hatred. There'll be no artisans, no clerks, no hewers of coal and minders of other men's machines.

That excerpt is from R.U.R. *(Rossum's Universal Robots), a play written by the Czech writer, Karel Čapek, in 1923. It was this play that brought the word 'robot' into our language.*
   This is how young Rossum set about inventing his robots.

Young Rossum said to himself: A man is something that, for instance, feels happy, plays the fiddle, likes going for walks, and, in fact, wants to do a whole lot of things that are really unnecessary. But a working machine must not want to play the fiddle, must not feel happy, must not do a whole lot of other things. A petrol motor must not have tassels or ornaments. Young Rossum invented a worker with the minimum amount of requirements. He had to simplify him. He rejected everything that did not contribute directly to the progress of work. In this way he rejected everything that makes man more expensive. In fact, he rejected man and made the Robot. Robots are not people. Mechanically they are more perfect than we are, they have an enormously developed intelligence, but they have no soul.

Karel Čapek

2: COMPASSION CIRCUIT

Another passage about robots. In this story, Janet is a human. She is being waited upon by her 'parlourmaid' robot, Hester.

The discussion point, whether human beings – despite their weaknesses – are more attractive than 'perfect' robots, might be followed up in the classroom.

'Thank you, Hester,' Janet said, as she leaned back against the cushion placed behind her. Not that it was necessary to thank a robot, but she had a theory that if you did not practise politeness with robots you soon forgot it with other people.

And, anyway, Hester was no ordinary robot. She was not even dressed as a parlourmaid any more. In four months she had become a friend, a tireless, attentive friend. From the first Janet had found it difficult to believe that she was only a mechanism, and as the days passed she had become more and more of a person. The fact that she consumed electricity instead of food came to seem little more than a foible.

'I suppose,' said Janet, settling back in her chair, 'that you must think me a poor, weak thing?'

Hester said, matter of factly:

'We were designed; you were just accidental. It is your misfortune, not your fault.'

'You'd rather be you than me?' asked Janet.

'Certainly,' Hester told her. 'We are stronger. We don't have to have frequent sleep to recuperate. We don't have to carry an unreliable chemical factory inside us. We don't have to grow old and deteriorate. Human beings are so clumsy and fragile and so often unwell because something is not working properly. If anything goes wrong with us, or is broken, it doesn't hurt and is easily replaced. And you have all kinds of words like pain, and suffering, and unhappiness, and weariness that we have to be taught to understand, and they don't seem to us to be useful things to have. I feel very sorry that you must have these things and be so uncertain and so fragile. It disturbs my compassion-circuit.'

'Oh no!' Janet protested. 'It can't be just that. You've a heart somewhere, Hester. You must have.'

'I expect it is more reliable than a heart,' said Hester.

John Wyndham

3: A MAN'S PLACE

A woman novelist's vision of the future, in which women establish themselves as the dominant sex. A father tries to persuade his rebellious son to conform.

'A man should be prepared to settle down to married life and concentrate on bringing up his children properly. What higher function in life could anyone ask?'

'The right to express himself?' Jimmy suggested. 'The right to work at what he's best fitted for?'

'Nobody's saying men shouldn't express themselves,' said his father, mildly. 'But they can do that without leaving the home and competing with women. A husband can take up music or poetry or writing – any of the arts in fact. If he wants physical exercise, there's nothing to stop him gardening, or playing tennis, or golf. But his chief duty is to make the home a place of peace and contentment for his wife and his children. . . . And it's all very well for you to shake your head, Jimmy, but more freedom wouldn't be a good thing at all.

'As things are, men may appear to have the subordinate role, but you and I know perfectly well they're often the power behind the throne. Most women admit that they owe their success in life at least in part to their husbands – and only the other day Mrs Hemingway, boss of General Manufacturers, was telling me that when she takes on a new executive, she insists on interviewing the husband, too. A woman's value to her organization is affected by the sort of husband she has – and a woman with an unreliable or unattractive husband just doesn't get the job.'

He turned to David. 'I tell you, Doctor Thornhill, what we have to remember is that men are the artists and the poets of the world – always have been, always will be. Women are the realists – the materialistic sex. So let them get on with the job of managing the world and leave the men at home with their dreams.'

Muriel Box

4: THE MACHINE

This passage is from a short story by E.M. Forster called The Machine Stops. *It is a prophecy of a future in which telecommunications have replaced human contact, a future that seems all the more likely than it did when the story was first published in 1947.*

Imagine, if you can, a small room, hexagonal in shape like the cell of a bee. An arm-chair is in the centre, by its side a reading-desk – that is all the furniture. And in the arm-chair there sits a woman, about five feet high, with a face as white as a fungus. It is to her that the little room belongs.

An electric bell rang.

The woman touched a switch and the music was silent. 'I suppose I must see who it is,' she thought, and set her chair in motion. The chair, like the music, was worked by machinery, and it rolled her to the other side of the room, where the bell still rang importunately.

'Who is it?' she called. Her voice was irritable, for she had been interrupted often since the music began. She knew several thousand people; in certain directions human intercourse had advanced enormously.

But when she listened into the receiver, her white face wrinkled into smiles, and she said. 'Very well. Let us talk, I will isolate myself. I do not expect anything important will happen for the next five minutes – for I can give you fully five minutes, Kuno.'

She touched the isolation knob, so that no one else could speak to her. The round plate she held in her hands began to glow, and presently she could see the image of her son, who lived on the other side of the earth, and he could see her.

'I have called you before, mother, but you were always busy or isolated. I have something particular to say.'

'What is it, dearest boy? Be quick. Why could you not send it by pneumatic post?'

'Because I prefer saying such a thing. I want –'

'Well?'

'I want you to come and see me.'

Vashti watched his face in the blue plate.

'But I can see you!' she exclaimed. 'What more do you want?'

'I want to see you not through the Machine,' said Kuno. 'I want to speak to you not through the wearisome Machine.'

'Oh, hush!' said his mother, vaguely shocked. 'You mustn't say anything against the Machine.'

'Why not?'

'One mustn't.'

'You talk as if a god had made the Machine,' cried the other. 'I believe that you pray to it when you are unhappy. Men made it, do not forget that. Great men, but men.'

E.M. Forster

5: MAN MAKES HIMSELF

Man inhabits two worlds. One is the natural world of plants and animals, of soils and airs and waters which preceded him by billions of years and of which he is a part. The other is the world of social institutions and artefacts he builds for himself, using his tools and engines, his science and his dreams to fashion an environment obedient to human purpose and direction.

The search for a better-managed human society is as old as man himself. It is rooted in the nature of human experience. Men believe they can be happy. They experience comfort, security, joyful participation, mental vigour, intellectual discovery, poetic insights, peace of soul, bodily rest. They seek to embody them in their human environment.

But the actual life of most of mankind has been cramped with back-breaking labour, exposed to deadly or debilitating disease, prey to wars and famines, haunted by the loss of children, filled with fear and the ignorance that breeds more fear. At the end, for everyone, stands dreaded unknown death. To long for joy, support and comfort, to react violently against fear and anguish is quite simply the human condition.

But today, as we enter the last decades of the twentieth century, there is a growing sense that something fundamental and possibly irrevocable is happening to man's relations with both his worlds.

In the last two hundred years, and with staggering acceleration in the last twenty-five, the power, extent and depth of man's interventions in the natural order seem to presage a revolutionary new epoch in human history, perhaps the most revolutionary which the mind can conceive. Men seem, on a planetary scale, to be substituting the controlled for the uncontrolled, the fabricated for the unworked, the planned for the random. And they are doing so with a speed and depth of intervention unknown in any previous age of human history.

Barbara Ward and René Dubois

10

Worship

———◆●◆●———

Many people believe that it is natural for human beings to worship, be it other human beings (sports or pop stars for example), material things, nature, or a divine being.

The idea of worship is explored in these five readings.

1: THE WIND IN THE WILLOWS

In one chapter of this famous book, two of the characters, Rat and Mole, paddle their boat up the river very early one morning. As the sun rises, they sense they are in the presence of some divine being, a god. In his presence, they feel it is natural to 'worship'.

Slowly, but with no doubt or hesitation whatever, and in something of a solemn expectancy, the two animals passed through the broken, tumultuous water and moored their boat at the flowery margin of the island. In silence they landed, and pushed through the blossom and scented herbage and undergrowth that led up to the level ground, till they stood on a little lawn of a marvellous green, set round with Nature's own orchard-trees – crab-apple, wild cherry, and sloe.

'This is the place of my song-dream, the place the music played to me,' whispered the Rat, as if in a trance. 'Here, in this holy place, here if anywhere, surely we shall find Him!'

Then suddenly the Mole felt a great Awe fall upon him, an awe that turned his muscles to water, bowed his head, and rooted his feet to the ground. It was no panic terror – indeed he felt wonderfully at peace and happy – but it was an awe that smote and held him and, without seeing, he knew it could only mean that some august Presence was very, very near. With difficulty he turned to look for his friend, and saw him at his side cowed, stricken, and

71

trembling violently. And still there was utter silence in the populous bird-haunted branches around them; and still the light grew and grew.

'Rat!' he found breath to whisper, shaking. 'Are you afraid?'

'Afraid?' murmured the Rat, his eyes shining with unutterable love. 'Afraid! Of *Him*? O, never, never! And yet – and yet – O, Mole, I am afraid!'

Then the two animals, crouching to the earth, bowed their heads and did worship.

Kenneth Grahame

2: FALSE GODS

The idols of this century are not those of history. These 'prayers' attempt to show the dangers of putting the wrong things first.

A prayer to television

Glory be to Ekco, peace to His Master's Voice and goodwill towards Pay TV.

We praise thee, we watch thee, we glorify thee.

O Telly, Varnished Box, Vital Tube.

O TV, the only begotten invention of Baird; O TV, Box of the Drawing Room, that takest away the boredom of humans, do not break down upon us.

O Box, that receiveth great pictures, do not crackle when we thy gogglers lift up our eyes to watch thy programmes. Forgive the scientists who equipped thee with an off switch, and grant that they may obtain redemption by giving us ever better versions of you.

But above all we thank thee for thine inestimably enjoyable pictures. Grant what we ask for thy industries' sake. Amen.

Mark Harrison (age 12)

Two prayers to the car

Most mighty and everpleasing car
Of a wondrous and superlative model
Which is sprung from a great make,
We will, every Sunday, wash you,
And if it is wonderful enough for you,
We will drive you over the smoothest roads

Which you have ever felt under your pneumatic tyres.
Amen.

Mark Vye (age 12)

O shining gleaming automobile,
That takest me from place to place
Whenever is my desire,
I confess to having sinned by leaving you
Outside in the Winter;
Forgive me, cleanse me from my sins,
And I will cleanse thy body of earthly grime.
Do not seize up when I drive slowly
For whenever there is no police car near
I will press the accelerator hard,
Sliding my foot to the clutch and changing gear
Until the speedometer needle reaches to the end of the
    scale.
I will endeavour at all times
To check your tyre pressures and clean your windscreen;
And if ever I forget, forgive me I pray,
For none except thy divine majesty is perfect.
I glorify, wash, tune and service thee,
I have faith in thy fuel consumption and acceleration,
    Glory be to thee, o divine automobile,
    Here and for many miles of happy motoring,
        Go Shell.

Stephen Dennison (age 13)

Exodus, chapter 32 *describes how Aaron disobeyed God (and Moses) by
making a false god, the golden calf.*

3: I AM DAVID

I Am David *is the story of a boy who escapes from a Communist prison
camp and sets out to find his home. He knows little about God but, as he
has heard many people talking about God in different ways, he believes
there are many gods. He himself believes in what he calls 'the God of the
green pastures and still waters'.*

*In this part of the story, he has just entered a church for the first time.
He is still afraid of being re-captured.*

The light inside was very subdued. David remained standing just inside the door until his eyes had grown accustomed to the change from the bright sunlight outside to the soft obscurity within.

It was very quiet. And beautiful. It reminded him a little of the house, though in many ways it was very different. There were paintings and carved woodwork and coloured glass in the windows. In front of some of the paintings along the side of the church candles were burning.

But the silence was not complete. David's eyes, now accustomed to the dim light, perceived a dark figure kneeling before one of the paintings. The man was saying something, very softly.

David crept quietly towards him. If it were someone praying, he wanted to listen. He might learn something. But he could not understand the words. It was . . . yes, it was Latin, and apart from a few words, he knew no Latin.

The figure rose. 'Good day, my son. Are you looking for something?'

'No, sir,' David replied politely. He stepped back hastily and glanced over his shoulder to make sure where the door lay.

'You need not be frightened of me. As you can see, I'm a priest.'

David realized he was right. Priests always wore long black gowns – outside the concentration camp. And a priest was never one of *them*. David ceased looking towards the door, and looked at the painting instead.

'Is that your God, sir?'

'No, that's Saint Christopher.'

'He's not a God?'

'There's only one God, my son.'

David frowned. That wasn't right; he *knew* there were several.

'What are you called, my son?'

'I'm David.'

'So you're David. And who's your God, David?'

'He's the God of the green pastures and the still waters . . .'

The priest looked at him and smiled. 'It's the same God.'

Anne Holm
(translated by L.W. Kingsland)

Psalm 23 *is the Bible passage which David had heard recited in the camp and on which he had based his belief.*

4: IN THE SYNAGOGUE

Jews worship in a synagogue. (Strictly speaking, the word 'synagogue' means the congregation and not the building, but it is regularly used to mean the building.)

The most important possession of any synagogue is the Torah, the first five books of the Old Testament.

In every Jewish synagogue the most prominent object is the ark, with a lamp burning perpetually before it. The ark is an ornamented cupboard, lined with curtains. It contains the scrolls of the Torah, hand written on parchment in Hebrew, and sometimes ornamented with bells, crowns and 'breastplates' of precious metal.

The high point in weekly worship comes on the Sabbath (Saturday) morning. The ark is opened and a scroll is lifted out and carried around the synagogue. Then there is a reading from it in the original Hebrew, normally chanted in ancient Jewish modes. Members of the congregation are 'called up' to recite blessings before and after the readings. At the end of the reading, the scroll is again carried around the synagogue: members may touch it with the fringes of their praying shawls and then they kiss the fringe. . . .

To an observant Jew, the Sabbath is not only a sacred but also a joyful day – it is common for Jews to wish one another a peaceful Sabbath. In one respect, it is one of Judaism's greatest gifts to the world. The Jews, and nobody else (in human terms), invented the idea of a weekly rest-day. Without them we might never have had the weekend. . . .

At thirteen, a Jewish boy becomes *bar mitzva*, that is, subject to the Law and is thereafter, for religious purposes, an adult. On the Sabbath after his thirteenth birthday he intones or reads publicly in the synagogue from the Torah for the first time. It can be a considerable ordeal, requiring a year's preparation. It can also be a deeply emotional occasion with his grandmothers weeping for joy. Customarily he receives his *tallith* (praying shawl) and his *siddur* (prayer book). Afterwards there is a party for family and friends. Nowadays there is also a *bat mitzvah* or confirmation ceremony for girls.

Colin Cross

Genesis, chapter 2, verses 2–3 *describe the institution of the Sabbath;*

how God showed his people that they must keep the Sabbath is described in Exodus, chapter 16, verses 22–30.

5: FIVE TIMES A DAY

The main Muslim prayer is the *salat*, which should be recited five times daily at set hours and according to a set formula. A devout individual will say other prayers at his own discretion, but the *salat*, according to strict teaching, is essential. It has been held that the *salat* is the regular awakening to reality: the rest of life is a mere dream.

The times of the *salat* are immediately before dawn, just after midday, late afternoon, just after sunset and when darkness has replaced twilight. In Islamic cities, the call to prayer goes out from the minarets of the mosques.

Traditionally the call is uttered by the *mu'adhdhin* ('muezzin') and it goes: 'God is great' (repeated four times), 'I witness that there is no God but God' (twice), 'I witness that Muhammad is the Prophet of God' (twice), 'Come to the *salat*' (twice), 'Come for success' (twice), 'There is no God but God.' 'God is great' (twice).

It takes about ten minutes to recite the *salat* and there is a fixed but simple ritual for it. At various stages the believer stands, crouches, kneels and prostrates himself. During the prostration he touches the ground with his forehead. Before starting the prayer he should wash himself. He should not allow himself to be interrupted. If, however, some worldly matter does intrude during the recitation, he must start again from the beginning.

Strictly, a mosque is not essential for the practice of Islam: what matters is the individual at prayer. A mosque is the place for communal prayer and instruction. Muslims are under a special duty to attend the mosque for midday prayer on a Friday, which Muhammad instituted as the Islamic holy day on somewhat the same lines as the Jewish Sabbath and the Christian Sunday. The social convention is that one should wear one's best clothes to the mosque on a Friday. One should also close one's business, at least during the hour of prayer. Attendance at the Friday service is for communal recitation of the *salat*, a sermon and discussion of community affairs. The convention is that a communal service in a mosque requires at least forty worshippers.

Women, in general, are not too much encouraged to attend the mosque. They should pray at home. If they do come to the mosque they should be segregated out of sight of the men.

The focal point of a mosque is the *mihrab*, a niche in the wall nearest to Mecca to which the congregation turns in prayer: it is often richly ornamented with abstract designs.

Colin Cross

11

Those who are different

————•◆•◆•————

1: LEPROSY SUFFERERS
(World Leprosy Day is the last Sunday in January)

Those who have leprosy are regarded as 'different' in some way from those who happen to have some other disease. They are still looked upon with fear or loathing in many countries, the West not excepted.

In some lands people with leprosy are still not allowed to own property, to attend school, to be admitted to a general hospital, to hold a job, or to remain at large. Leprosy may be legal grounds for divorce. Many are denied elementary human rights by their families or by the law.

But leprosy can be cured.

Babu was sitting at the end of a bench in a hospital in South India. His face was solemn, and thoughtful, for he was engaged on a most important task: he was learning how to pinch.

Although he was only about eleven, Babu had had leprosy for some years, and the main nerve of his arm had been damaged by the disease. The result was that the fingers of that hand had become clawed. (Hold *your* hand and half close all the fingers so that they look like claws. Keep them in that position and try to pick up a pen; you will find it almost impossible.)

Fortunately, Babu had been taken to a village clinic for treatment. He went every week without fail for three whole years, and every week he swallowed two small white tablets. Slowly the patches on his skin cleared up. He was cured of leprosy. But his fingers remained curled and bent.

He was admitted to hospital. For several weeks, he had to do exercises with his fingers to make them supple again. Every day, his hand was put into a bath of warm wax which helped to soften the skin. Then, when the doctor thought that his hand was ready,

Babu had an operation. The tendon of a strong muscle in the forearm was split into four 'tails', and each little 'tail' was burrowed under the skin of a finger and stitched in place so as to take over the work of the weak muscle. After a fortnight, when the bandages and the plaster had been removed, Babu had to learn how to use his fingers again. He persevered with his exercises, until he could actually pinch, that is, he could bring together the tips of his thumb and index finger and pick up small objects.

But Babu had something else to worry about. Leprosy had also attacked the nerves of his face, so that the small muscles were paralysed. Babu could not shut his eyes, even when he was asleep. The surgeon was able to correct even this. He took a small part of the muscle that helps to close the mouth, and threaded it just under the eyelid. He then did the same operation on the other eye. When the stitches had been removed, Babu was told to practise biting hard, closing his mouth with a snap. As he did so, his eyes would shut.

The Leprosy Mission

Matthew, chapter 8, verses 1–4. *These verses tell how Jesus healed a leprosy sufferer.* (See also **Mark**, chapter 1, verses 40–5; *and* **Luke**, chapter 5, verses 12–15.)
  The Old Testament laws about the way leprosy was to be regarded can be found in **Leviticus**, chapter 14. *The story of Elisha healing Naaman is told in* II **Kings**, chapter 5.

2: MORE ABOUT LEPROSY

What is it?
Leprosy is a disease that damages the skin, the nerves of the limbs and the face, and the lining of the nose. It is caused by a tiny germ.
Where is it found?
In nearly every country in the world, especially in the hot countries of Africa, Asia and South America.
Is it very catching?
No, not very. But many people fear leprosy, and think that it can be caught easily.
How is it caught?
Usually by living in close contact with someone who has the

catching kind of leprosy. Close contact generally means living in an overcrowded house. Discharge from the nose is probably the commonest source of infection.

How many people have leprosy?
Probably about fifteen million, which means about one in every 200 in the world. (What would that be in your school or your street?) Of course, leprosy is not spread evenly throughout the world, and in countries where there is a lot of leprosy, there may be many districts where there is little or none. There are villages in Africa and India in which over half the people have leprosy; everybody seems to catch it sooner or later. Fortunately, where the disease is most rife, many patients have the kind of leprosy that cures itself. Those who work to cure leprosy do not use the word 'leper' for somebody who is suffering from leprosy, because this word is often associated with ideas of uncleanness and even of wrong-doing. It hurts innocent people who happen to have caught leprosy.

Should patients with leprosy be segregated?
No. Segregation leads to concealment of leprosy, especially of leprosy in its early infectious and curable stages. Segregation does not in practice stamp out leprosy.

How can leprosy be recognized?
The first symptom is commonly an area of skin numbness or a feeling of 'pins and needles'. The first sign is usually some local-ized change in the same area: the skin slowly loses its colour and feeling, sweating and hair growth may be impaired. Leprosy germs may be either very numerous or extremely scanty in such a patch. The early signs and symptoms of leprosy may be mistaken for any of a number of skin diseases.

Can leprosy be cured?
Yes. Patients with a high degree of resistance can be cured with-out much difficulty, and they do not relapse. Other patients take longer to cure, and live germs may lurk deep in the body when they are no longer to be found in the skin. There are several drugs that kill leprosy germs, but it takes longer for the body to get rid of dead leprosy germs than for medicines to kill the living germs.

What drugs are available for the treatment of leprosy?
The drug most commonly used in the treatment of leprosy is diamino-diphenyl-sulphone (DDS or dapsone). It is given by

mouth or by injection. The drug itself is not expensive. Other drugs are available where dapsone cannot be given.

Jesus told his disciples to 'Heal the sick, cleanse the lepers' (*St Matthew, chapter 10, verse 8*). Since 1874 The Leprosy Mission has worked with the Christian Churches to fulfil this command, giving physical and spiritual help to leprosy sufferers.

How does it work?
When the work began there was no cure for leprosy, but sufferers were given shelter, food, clothing and the ministry of the Gospel. Today, medicine, physiotherapy, surgery and vocational training are all used in fighting the disease and in preparing healed patients to return to normal life in the community. Increasingly, help is being taken to patients at home in their villages, where early cases may be found and treated, and the spread of disease prevented.

British Leprosy Association

If you are choosing leprosy for a classroom project or if you want to know more about leprosy, write to the Leprosy Mission (50 Portland Place, London W1N 3DG). Also available is Project, *a magazine for younger pupils.*

The Leprosy Mission is international and interdenominational. All patients are treated without distinction, whether they are Christians or not.

3: ECZEMA

Thousands of children suffer from a skin complaint called eczema. Though it is very common, little is known about it and, like so many problems, it is not until you experience it that you realize the agonies involved.

In this passage, a mother describes what it was like for her eight-year-old son when he was suffering from eczema.

Think of dozens of gnat bites all over your body: in your hair, on your legs, round your eyes, between your fingers – burning, irritating, scratched raw. Then you get somewhere near what the eczema sufferer often puts up with night and day, year in and year out.

Eczema varies in degrees. It may be just a temporary upset of a baby's skin which passes when he reaches three. For some it means the odd recurring dry patch on the cheek or behind the knee. For others it means being covered from head to foot in itching sores.

For our son Adam, aged eight and a half, eczema has meant a life of almost constant discomfort. Even when the rash is at its least troublesome it's still there underneath, waiting to erupt at the least provocation.

There is no cure, only attempts at prevention by keeping the sufferer away from anything that might make him worse. After that it's a matter of ointments and creams which, if you're lucky, keep the eczema under control.

There is something about a skin ailment that repels people, however hard they would deny this. Possibly they are afraid of contamination because they see it as in some way dirty. Possibly they are afraid of catching it like measles. Eczema is not contagious. But you can't rush up explaining this to strangers at swimming pools as they gaze goggle-eyed at the scabby legs and spotted back.

At its worst, particularly on the face, the rash seems to distort skin and features. Eyes swell, the nose appears to thicken, the mouth cakes with encrusted sores. Add to this the cracking flaking dryness and you see an almost unrecognizable mask. One day Adam ran in from the street having caught sight of his face in a car mirror. In tears, he felt unable to go out and play any more. During another particularly bad patch, when he was five, he gazed down at his almost raw legs and wished he were dead, that he was a skeleton.

Christine Orton

Christine Orton concluded her description (which was published in the Guardian *newspaper) with these words, 'Perhaps we should form a society for the sufferers and their relatives. Then what information there is can be exchanged and circulated. The need, after all, must be great.'*

As a result of her article, the National Eczema Society was formed to help sufferers and their families.

For further details of the National Eczema Society, write to the General Secretary, at 5–7 Tavistock Place, London WC1H 9SR, enclosing a stamped addressed envelope.

4: JAKE

It is very easy to patronize the blind, believing that because they are blind, they must be 'different' in some way. Obviously they are limited, but that does not mean they should live a life apart, as this news item reminds us:

Some blind people may boycott the scented garden to be planted in Regent's Park, London, because they feel it 'smacks of segregation'. Mr George Miller, a blind journalist, said yesterday: 'If the public sees blind people feeling and smelling plants and flowers they will think, "Oh, the poor things, they are blind." This is just the sort of sympathy we do not want.'

The following passage is part of a story about a blind boy, called Jake.

One morning when Jake was five he had lain for a while listening to bird sounds and traffic sounds and decided that it would be a good hour before anyone else was up, so he'd slipped downstairs to the kitchen for a cup of milk.

He'd taken his mug off its special hook and was opening the fridge when he'd realized that there was someone else in the room. Not Mum – she'd have started talking. Not Dad – there'd have been cigarette smoke. His brother Martin never got up till he had to. No, there was a stranger sitting by the table, watching him.

Jake turned with the bottle in his hand and said, 'Who are you? What are you doing in our house?'

'You're Jake,' said a quiet, slow voice.

'Who are you?' said Jake.

'I'm your grandfather.'

'No you aren't. Granpa's across the sea.'

'They made me come home. They didn't give me time to write to your Mum'.

Jake felt for the mug he'd left on top of the fridge, poured it two-thirds full of milk and put the bottle back. He could feel Granpa watching him all the time. He was proud of the way he did things for himself – several of his sighted friends weren't allowed to pour out their own milk because their Mums thought they'd spill – so he didn't mind showing off to Granpa.

'Shall I tell you a story about crocodiles?' asked Granpa suddenly.

'A true story?'

'I don't make things up, Jake.'

'All right. I'll go and fetch my dressing gown.'

When Jake came down again the kitchen was empty. He found his milk and went to the lounge. It smelt of bedrooms, as if somebody had been sleeping on the sofa, but Granpa was standing over by the window, watching him again.

'You can sit down,' said Jake. 'But you mustn't put your feet on the chairs.'

'I thought you couldn't see anything at all, Jake.'

'Course I can't. And I won't ever, either. I don't mind.'

'How did you know I was here?'

'I just knew.'

Peter Dickinson

5: SHAME

Many people feel ashamed, not because they are 'different' in a physical way, such as suffering from leprosy or eczema, but because they do not conform to an accepted social pattern.

In this memory of childhood some years ago, the writer, Lesley Davies, remembers a particularly hurtful remark.

Once, when I was about nine my father lost his job and couldn't get another one. We were evicted from our house and sent to live in the poor ward of a local hospital. This ward contained about a hundred beds divided from each other by grey blankets hung on ropes. It was full of women and children. No fathers were allowed. Mine slept in the park and got shaved in the public lavatory every day. I was terribly ashamed of living in the hospital. I had always thought poor old loonies went there, not ordinary people like us. Every afternoon I used to sneak the long way round coming from school so nobody would see where I lived. I know it shouldn't have mattered to me but it did. Anyway one day this girl in my class, Jean Meredith, followed me home. I didn't see her but next day everyone in my class knew I lived in the hospital. I tried to pretend I didn't care but just a few odd remarks to the girl sitting next to me about being careful what she caught really hurt. I couldn't wait for the day to end and I thought I would never go back to that school again even if I had to play truant every day.

Those who are different

That afternoon we had English and we were reading a play. Our class teacher, Miss Sansom, picked people to go to the front of the class and act it. She told me to read Dick Whittington. The part of the play we did that afternoon was where he was on the road to London in his rags. He feels hopeless and decides to give up the idea of going to London, and return home. I suppose I read it with feeling because I was poor too and life was looking pretty hopeless for me. When Miss Sansom rang the classroom bell, pretending to be the bells of London and one of the boys said, 'Turn again, Whittington, Lord Mayor of London', I was overcome with joy. It seemed like it was really me it was happening to. Then the lesson finished and I was just me again, still humiliated. Before she started the next lesson Miss Sansom held her hand up for silence. 'Lesley,' she said. 'Have you ever thought of being an actress when you grow up? I think you'd be a very good one.' Everybody looked at me. I went bright red. I thought it was like Dick Whittington hearing the bells, but this time it really was for me. What she said didn't change anything: I still had to go home to the hospital. But that day and many days after I walked home with a wonderful feeling inside me.

Lesley Davies

12
Modern parables

1: THE GLASS IN THE FIELD

A short time ago some builders, working on a studio in Connecticut, left a huge square of plate glass standing upright in a field one day. A goldfinch flying swiftly across the field struck the glass and was knocked cold. When he came to he hastened to his club, where an attendant bandaged his head and gave him a stiff drink.

'What the hell happened?' asked a sea gull.

'I was flying across a meadow when all of a sudden the air crystallized on me.' said the goldfinch.

The sea gull, and a hawk, and an eagle all laughed heartily. A swallow listened gravely.

'For fifteen years, fledgling and bird, I've flown this country,' said the eagle, 'and I assure you there is no such thing as air crystallizing. Water, yes; air, no.'

'You were probably struck by a hailstone,' said the sea gull. 'What do you think, swallow?'

'Why, I – I think maybe the air crystallized on him,' said the swallow. The large birds laughed so loudly that the goldfinch became annoyed and bet them each a dozen worms that they couldn't follow the course he had flown across the field without encountering the hardened atmosphere. They all took his bet; the swallow went along to watch. The sea gull, the eagle, and the hawk decided to fly together over the route the goldfinch indicated.

'You come too,' they said to the swallow.

'I – I – well, no,' said the swallow. 'I don't think I will.'

So the three large birds took off together and they hit the glass together and they were all knocked cold.

Moral: He who hesitates is sometimes saved.

James Thurber

2: UNEXPECTED GOOD FORTUNE

Once upon a time there was a man who did nothing all day long – he just waited and hoped that suddenly he would meet with unexpected good fortune and become rich in an instant without any effort.

And thus he lived for many a year, until one day he heard tell that there was a certain island inhabited by people who had only one eye.

'At last. That will be my good fortune,' thought the man to himself. 'I'll travel to that island. I'll catch one of these one-eyed creatures and bring him back and show him in the market place for a penny a look. In a short while I shall be a rich man.'

And the more he thought about it, the more he liked the idea.

Finally he made up his mind. He sold the little that he had, bought a boat and set off. After a long journey he reached the island of the one-eyed creatures and, indeed, hardly had he stepped ashore when he saw that the people there really had only one eye each. But of course the one-eyed people noticed that here was a man with two eyes, and a few of them got together and said: 'At last! So this will be our good fortune. Let's catch him and show him in the market-place for a penny a look. We'll soon be rich men!!'

No sooner said than done. They seized the two-eyed man and carried him off to the market-place, where they showed him for a penny a look. And that's the sort of thing that happens to people who look for unexpected good fortune.

Traditional

3: IN THE DOLDRUMS

This story comes from a book called The Phantom Tollbooth *which is about the adventures of a boy called Milo, who travels in his car to a number of unlikely places, sometimes without thinking.* . . .

As Milo drove along the peaceful road he soon fell to day-dreaming and paid less and less attention to where he was going. In a short time he wasn't paying any attention at all and that is why, at a fork in the road, when a sign pointed to the left, Milo went to the right, along a route which looked suspiciously like the wrong way.

Things began to change as soon as he left the main highway. The sky became quite grey and, along with it, the whole countryside seemed to lose its colour and assume the same monotonous tone. Everything was quiet, and even the air hung heavily. The birds sang only grey songs and the road wound back and forth in an endless series of climbing curves.

'It looks as though I'm getting nowhere,' yawned Milo, becoming very drowsy and dull. 'I hope I haven't taken a wrong turn.'

Mile after

mile after

mile after

mile, and everything became greyer and more monotonous. Finally, the car just stopped altogether, and, hard as he tried, it wouldn't budge another inch.

'I wonder where I am,' said Milo in a very worried tone.

'You're . . . in . . . the . . . Dol . . . drums,' wailed a voice that sounded far away.

'WHAT ARE THE DOLDRUMS?' he cried loudly, and tried very hard to see who would answer this time.

'The Doldrums, my young friend, are where nothing ever happens and nothing ever changes.'

So Milo got stuck in the Doldrums. And the only way of getting out of the Doldrums is to start thinking. Just as Tock (who's a watch dog) helps Milo to do.

'I suppose you know why you got stuck,' said Tock.

'I suppose I just wasn't thinking,' said Milo.

'PRECISELY,' shouted the dog, 'and since you got here by not thinking, it seems reasonable to expect that, in order to get out, you must start thinking.'

Milo began to think as hard as he could (which was very difficult, since he wasn't used to it). He thought of birds that swim and fish that fly. He thought of yesterday's lunch and tomorrow's dinner. And, as he thought, the wheels began to turn.

'We're moving, we're moving,' he shouted happily.

'Keep thinking,' said the watchdog.

Norton Juster

4: THE SHORE AND THE SEA

A single excited lemming started the exodus, crying 'Fire!' and running towards the sea. He may have seen the sunrise through the trees, or waked from a fiery nightmare, or struck his head against a stone, producing stars. Whatever it was, he ran and ran, and as he ran he was joined by others, a mother lemming and her young, a night-watch lemming on his way home to bed, and assorted revellers and early risers.

'The world is coming to an end!' they shouted, and as the hurrying hundreds turned into thousands, the reasons for their headlong flight increased by leaps and bounds and hops and skips and jumps.

'The devil has come in a red chariot!' cried an elderly male. 'The sun is his torch! The world is on fire!'

'It's a pleasure jaunt,' squeaked an elderly female.

'A what?' she was asked.

'A treasure hunt!' cried a wild-eyed male who had been up all night. 'Full many a gem of purest ray serene the dark unfathomed caves of ocean bear.'

'It's a bear!' shouted his daughter. 'Go it!'

And there were those among the fleeing thousands who shouted 'Goats!' and 'Ghosts!' until there almost as many different alarms as there were fugitives.

One male lemming who had lived alone for many years refused to be drawn into the stampede that swept past his cave like a flood. He saw no flames in the forest, and no devil, or bear, or goat, or ghost. He had long ago decided, since he was a serious scholar, that the caves of ocean bear no gems, but only soggy glub and great gobs of mucky gump. And so he watched the other lemmings leap into the sea and disappear beneath the waves, some crying 'We are saved!' and some crying 'We are lost!' The scholarly lemming shook his head sorrowfully, tore up what he had written through the years about his species and started his studies all over again.

Moral: All men should strive to learn before they die what they are running from, and to, and why.

James Thurber

5: GENESIS

'Who are you?' said the Prime Minister, opening the door.

'I am God,' replied the stranger.

'I don't believe you,' sneered the Prime Minister. 'Show me a miracle.'

And God showed the Prime Minister the miracle of birth.

'Pah,' said the Prime Minister. 'My scientists are creating life in test-tubes and have nearly solved the secret of heredity. Artificial insemination is more certain than your lackadaisical method, and by cross-breeding we are producing fish and mammals to our design. Show me a proper miracle.'

And God caused the sky to darken and hailstones came pouring down.

'That's nothing,' said the Prime Minister, picked up the telephone to the Air Ministry. 'Send up a met. plane would you, old chap, and sprinkle the clouds with silver chloride crystals.'

And the met. plane went up and sprinkled the clouds which had darkened the world and the hailstones stopped pouring down and the sun shone brightly.

'Show me another,' said the Prime Minister.

And God caused a plague of frogs to descend upon the land.

The Prime Minister picked up his telephone. 'Get the Min. of Ag. and Fish,' he said to the operator, 'and instruct them to procure a frog-killer as myxomatosis killed rabbits.'

And soon the land was free of frogs, and the people gave thanks to the Prime Minister and erected laboratories in his name.

'Show me another,' sneered the Prime Minister.

And God caused the sea to divide.

The Prime Minister picked up his direct-link telephone to the Polaris submarine. 'Lob a few ICBMs into Antarctica and melt the ice-cap, please, old man.'

And the ice-cap melted into water and the sea came rushing back.

'I will kill all the first-born,' said God.

'Paltry tricks,' said the Prime Minister. 'Watch this.' He pressed the button on his desk. And missiles flew to their preordained destinations and H-bombs split the world asunder and radioactivity killed every mortal thing.

'I can raise the dead,' said God.

'Please,' said the Prime Minister in his cardboard coffin. 'Let me live again.'

'Why, who are you?' said God, closing the lid.

Brian Morris

13
Money

1: WHAT IS MONEY?

Amongst primitive tribes there was no need for money. They were able to grow and hunt the food and make the clothes and shelter their simple wants required. Some people, however, were probably better at some jobs – say making pots or hunting animals – than others were and they would spend most of their time on what they could do best. Money would still not be needed. Just as a schoolboy swaps his unwanted stamps for somebody else's unwanted marbles so the man who made pots would swap a pot for a piece of meat with the man who hunted. Both would be satisfied. This swapping is called barter and was the basis of early trade.

You can imagine, however, that as a society developed, to barter the direct exchange of goods and services between person and person (a man might swap a pot for a visit from the witch doctor), would become impossibly complicated. For example, you, a tent maker, require some sandals immediately but you haven't a tent ready to swap. When you have it will be worth many pairs of sandals and you only want one pair. What can be done? Some convenient and fair way of swapping and also of 'giving change' must be found and that's where money came in.

At first money was not coins and notes but something the tribe valued, cattle for instance. If a man wanted a new wife or canoe he paid for it in cattle. He sold his goods and services for cattle (money), knowing that he in his turn could get what he wanted by offering cattle (money) in exchange.

What is money for? The answer is, first, that it makes swapping easier. Second, it acts as a measure of value, a price tag; for example, a canoe is worth so many head of cattle, a wife so many more.

It came to be thought that whatever was used for money should be easily carried, lasting, and valuable in itself. Bulls and cows won't do: gold and silver are much better. Today for practical purposes their place has been taken by notes, which in themselves are only worth the paper they're printed on.

We are willing to take our weekly wage in paper notes because the use of money is based on confidence and trust. We are prepared to give up something of value we possess (something we have, or have made, or can do) in exchange for money, only because we believe that we will find people ready to do the same when we want something. Money, then, is confidence and the use of paper money, in particular, is an act of faith.

Jack Singleton

2: MR MICAWBER

'Annual income twenty pounds, annual expenditure nineteen pounds nineteen and six, result happiness. Annual income twenty pounds, annual expenditure twenty pounds nought and six, result misery.'

That famous statement about money and happiness is uttered by Mr Micawber, in Charles Dickens' novel David Copperfield. *Micawber is usually in debt; but he rarely allows his poverty to get him down – or not for long at any rate. In this excerpt from the novel, David Copperfield describes what happens when one of Mr Micawber's creditors calls to try to collect the money he is owed.*

One dirty-faced man, I think he was a boot-maker, used to edge himself into the passage as early as seven o'clock in the morning, and call up the stairs to Mr Micawber – 'Come! You ain't out yet, you know. Pay us, will you? Don't hide, you know; that's mean. I wouldn't be mean if I was you. Pay us, will you? You just pay us, d'ye hear? Come!'

Receiving no answer to these taunts, he would mount in his wrath to the words 'swindlers' and 'robbers'; and these being ineffectual too, would sometimes go to the extremity of crossing the street, and roaring up at the windows of the second floor, where he knew Mr Micawber was. At these times, Mr Micawber would be transported with grief and mortification, even to the length of making motions at himself with a razor; but within half an hour afterwards, he would polish up his shoes with extraordinary pains, and go out, humming a tune with a greater air of gentility then ever.

Mr Micawber was either being completely irresponsible, or very properly refusing to be bowed down by money worries.
   In the same book, we get a glimpse of what it is like to be really short of cash, when David Copperfield himself starts work.

My breakfast was a penny loaf and a pennyworth of milk. I kept another small loaf, and a modicum of cheese, on a particular shelf of a particular cupboard, to make my supper on when I came back at night. This made a hole in the six or seven shillings, I know well, and I was out at the warehouse all day, and had to support myself on that money all the week. Often, in going to Murdstone and Grinby's, of a morning, I could not resist the stale pastry put out for sale at half-price at the pastrycook's doors, and spent in that, the money I should have kept for my dinner. Then, I went without my dinner.

   I remember two pudding-shops, between which I was divided, according to my finances. One was in a court close to St Martin's Church. The pudding at this shop was made of currants, and was rather a special pudding, but was dear, twopennyworth not being larger than a pennyworth of more ordinary pudding. A good shop for the latter was in the Strand – somewhere in that part which has been rebuilt since. It was a stout, pale pudding, heavy and flabby, and with only a few flat raisins in it.

Charles Dickens

3: UNFAIR DISTRIBUTION

Many people have lamented the unfair distribution of wealth, and that while the rich stay rich, the poor stay poor.

It is extraordinary how the everyday pursuit of money, in which we are all engaged, has somehow come to be regarded as purely practical, a cold, calculating business that has nothing to do with dreams.

   Yet the fact is that nearly all of us have one or two dreams about money. One dream is that when we are rich we shall live more gaudy, more exotic, happier lives; the other conceives of life as a series of concentric platforms, all revolving in the same direction, but at varying speeds, the fastest on the outside. To be poor is to be on the outside circle, where all the goods you acquire are flung off by sheer centrifugal force. You have a job to stay on the platform yourself, let alone hold on to a lot of parcels. You find, for instance, that you have got to have a new pair of shoes, so you rush into a shop and buy some, some cheap ones, and they are worn out in three months. But if you were on one of the inner platforms you would go calmly into a rather splendid shop and buy the sort of shoes that are bought by men on leave in London from Africa, or down from the Scottish moorland estates. Twenty years later these men are still wearing the same shoes; and the point is that after these twenty years inner-circle men have spent far less on shoes than outside men.

Paul Jennings

Matthew, chapter 20, verses 1–16 *is the Parable of the Labourers in the Vineyard and is Jesus' teaching that we should not be envious of others. Approximately three quarters of his parables involve money.*

4: A PRAYER FOR PAGANS

This meditation comes from an Australian book called Prayers for Pagans.

Lord, I have been counting my money.
I have to with the cost of living what it is.
And I have a family to keep too, you know.
Now let me see, Lord:
   There are the house payments –
   (Thank goodness they haven't increased)
Then there's the TV instalment, another two dollars a week.
   The boys' school books.
O yes, daughter's party dress.
There seems to be no end to expenses this week.
I tried to make a few extra dollars on the poker machine,
   Lord.
You know what happened. I did six bucks cold.
That means my shoes wait another week.
   Then there's the percolator, Lord, my wife's been on
   about that for days.
   And she hasn't a thing to wear.

How is it, Lord, every time I look at the cheque book there's
   so little there?
And how about those with no money at all, Lord,
   or the pensioners?
People battling day to day, waiting for pension day to come?
It's only when I look at others, Lord, I begin to see how rich I
   am.
Seen the slums? The soup kitchen lineups?
The city missions? The barefoot ragged kids in the park?
   The wealth is yours, Lord.
The glittering gold that backs the dollars and cents
   we use each day.
How have we messed up the distribution?
What sort of steward have I been of the wealth you've given
   me?
Help me confess my carelessness.
What have I offered you, Lord,
   Not in cash, perhaps, but:
   In honesty in my dealing?
   In trusteeship?
Teach me, Lord, that I am using your bounty.
   Your gifts,
And bless me as I become aware of
   my responsibility.   Amen.

Roger Bush

5: THE £5 NOTE

*Money can serve or destroy man. This reading illustrates this point and
is adapted from a 'Prayer before a five pound note'. The reader may feel its
points are made more effectively if he or she is holding an actual (used)
banknote.*

It will never tell all it hides in its creases.
It will never reveal all the struggles and efforts it represents,
   all the disillusionment and slighted dignity.
It is laden with all the weight of the human toil which makes
   its worth.
It has offered white roses to the radiant fiancée.
It has paid for the baptismal party, and fed the growing
   baby.

It has provided bread for the family table.
Because of it there was laughter among the young, and joy
  among the adults.
It has paid for the saving visit of the doctor.
It has bought the book that taught the youngster,
It has clothed the young girl.

But it has sent the letter breaking the engagement.
It has paid for the death of a child in its mother's womb.
It has bought the liquor that made the drunkard.
It has produced the film unfit for children.
And has recorded the indecent song.
It has broken the morals of the adolescent and made of the
  adult a thief.
It has bought for a few hours the body of a woman.
It has paid for the weapons of the crime and for the wood of
  the coffin.
This note has joyous mysteries, and sorrowful mysteries.
It is a symbol of all the labours of men, which tomorrow will
  be changed into eternal life.

Michel Quoist

14
Work

—◦—◦—

Five readings about jobs and careers, and the experience of work.

1: THE INTERVIEW

The interview does not always turn out as planned. The storyteller in this passage is applying for a job at a locomotive shed on the railway with a view to one day becoming a train driver.
He has been told to report to Mr Bidwell.

I went straight up to the door and I gave a good firm knock on it.
'Come in,' called a voice.
I turned the door-handle and went in. It was more like a small workshop than an office. There were lots of plans and blueprints around the place, and also some engineer's fine tools hanging from shelves. Mr Bidwell was standing beside his desk. He was a round-faced man and not nearly as frightening as I had imagined. I put on a special big smile for him.
'Good morning, sir,' I called out in a loud voice.
'Good morning, laddie,' he said. I could see he was rather pleased at my smiling appearance, as though he wasn't used to people smiling at him.
'I've come for a job, sir,' I said. He was going to say something but I thought it might be better if I said all my piece at once. 'I don't care how low I start, sir. I'll soon work my way up. And what's more, I can start this very minute.'
In that moment I could see that I had won him. He was an elderly man, grown old before his time, I decided, and he wasn't at all the ogre he had been made out to be. He was smiling warmly at me and I realized the job was mine. I pictured myself on the footplate of the Flying Scotsman on my first long trip, with

my mum and dad in the first-class compartment behind. Although he was smiling there seemed to be a hint of sadness in that smile. I'll cheer him up, I thought, as we work together.

'Now on what job, sir,' I said, 'would you like me to start?'

He hesitated. 'I'm not sure,' he said. 'It's not for me to say, not rightly.'

'Oh, but it is,' I said. 'I'll do anything you tell me.'

He shook his head. 'I think it'd be better,' he said, 'if you were to wait and see Mr Bidwell.'

I could hardly believe my ears. 'M-mister who?'

'Mr Bidwell,' he said. 'I'm only the sweeper-up.'

Bill Naughton

2: CHILD LABOUR

In the nineteenth century, many young children went to work, not to school. Those who nowadays wish the law allowed them to work longer hours in spare-time jobs (if they can find them) might reflect that these laws were made for their protection.

It is unlikely that they will be repealed while there is unemployment, but would young people really like them to be abolished? Or would that mean a return to the days of exploitation?

What made the child labour of the nineteenth century so horrible was, in the first place, that children did not choose and could not refuse to do it. They were almost literally slaves, pressed into labour by their parents, themselves so dreadfully poor that without little money brought in by the labour of the child they could not have kept the family alive. Half-starved already, had the child not worked, he would have starved altogether. But if he was a slave he was no more so than his parents, and, like them, he had no choice about what work he could do. He could not shop around, bargain, wait for something to turn up. He had to take what was offered when it was offered.

The next thing that made child labour terrible was the work itself. It was too hard, too demanding, too much for the child's strength. It went on too long: fourteen and even sixteen hour days were not uncommon. And it was done too often in terribly unhealthy and dangerous conditions. But all of this was as true for adults as for the child. The mines and the mills and the sweat-shops were no less horrible for them. They too were mangled in machinery, poisoned by dust and chemicals, killed in accidents, drained of their health and strength. Women sewing in the garment shops of New York often lost their sight. One particularly dreadful statistic comes back to me. The economist and industrial consultant Peter Drucker once wrote that the average working life of the migrant labourers who built our great railroads was *five years*. This compares very well with the destructiveness of Stalin's slave labour camps, about which we have been so indignant. Our modern economy, like the economy of most great industrial nations, was built no less than Russia's on human bones and blood.

Finally, children were exploited because, like their parents, they were grossly underpaid for their work and because, since it was needed for the family, they could not keep or use any of the money they earned.

John Holt

3: ANOTHER INTERVIEW

Is this a fair way of selecting a man for a job?

Waiting in a steamship office to be interviewed for a job as wireless operator, a group of applicants filled the room with such a buzz of conversation that they were oblivious to the dots and dashes which began coming over the loudspeaker.

About this time another man entered and sat down quietly by himself. Suddenly he jumped to attention, walked into the private office, and then came out smiling.

'Here,' one of the group called out, 'how did you get in ahead of us? We were here first.'

'One of you would have got the job,' he replied, 'if you'd listened to the message from the loudspeaker.'

'What message?' they asked in surprise.

'Why, the morse code,' the stranger answered. 'It said: "The man I need must always be on the alert. The man who gets this message and comes directly into my private office will be placed on one of my ships as an operator." '

Walter C. Mello

4: TRADE UNIONS

When you start work you enter a great heritage. Men and women before you have sweated and suffered, some even died, so that you can enjoy the wages and conditions of work that you will find. You may not think they are good enough; that you will still not get a fair share of the wealth your skill and strength will create for your employer. The union at one level or another will negotiate with him for better pay and prospects. Such negotiation is called collective bargaining.

Collective agreements may be about overtime, meal breaks, workshop practice, the rate for the job, engagement of workers and so on. If you are wrongly dismissed from work your union may take up your case in law.

Many unions have unemployment, sickness and death benefits, pension schemes, convalescent homes and other ways of catering for the welfare of members. Most provide opportunities for further education in political, economic and trade union subjects; organize day and weekend conferences; and give scholarships to attend colleges.

In some firms and industries management and workers get together from time to time to discuss how to improve output in what are called working parties or joint production councils. The unions usually supply the workers' representatives on such bodies.

A member can expect a great deal from his trade union, but much also is expected of him (or her) in return.

First of all you are expected to pay your dues. That goes without saying. Headquarters have to be maintained, a fund built up from which to draw strike pay, and welfare facilities provided. There is one possible payment that needs explaining – the political levy. Trade unions have the power to use some of their funds for political purposes. The members vote for the particular purpose this money shall support, for instance, trade union candidates for parliament. If a member does not want to pay the political levy he contracts out, that is he signs a declaration to that effect.

A trade union is democratic and a member should attend his branch meeting to elect officers and delegates and discuss action. It is because some members are lazy and apathetic that in some unions extremists have been elected to key positions. The members of a union (or unions) in a particular firm also elect their own shop stewards. Remember that if you work in a factory the shop steward is your personal representative on the shop floor dealing with the day-to-day situations that may arise between you and the management.

If the union declares an official strike (in recent years there have been unofficial strikes called by irresponsible shop stewards), because negotiations with the employer have reached a stalemate you are expected to stop work. If you are an apprentice, however, you will probably have agreed in your indentures not to take part in a labour dispute. No sensible person likes a strike, as it uses up union funds, causes bad blood, slows down national life, and it is only used as a last weapon. Occasionally to press a point a token strike of a day may be called.

Those who stay at work when a strike is on are dubbed 'scabs' or 'blacklegs'. They may be deprived of their union membership card, which can be very serious, as in some places it is their only passport to employment. Such factories or firms that will only engage union members are known as 'closed shops'. The principle behind the 'closed shop' is that it is unfair for a non-union worker to share the benefits obtained largely through the work of the unions. He is looked upon as a parasite, 'a man who goes through a swing door without pushing'.

Jack Singleton

5: MR WILLIAM HUDSON, J.P.

The man who 'gets on' is not always admirable.

William Hudson, Justice of the Peace, Certificate of the British Emporium, was a small man with big dreams. He was king of the district. He owned everything in sight and what he didn't own was owed to him. He was a great one for collecting, particularly people and their businesses. Yet the more he collected, the smaller he seemed to feel and, as there was a strong streak of masochism in him, he would not stop collecting till he starved to death. He had come up from nothing and that's what he wanted to return to; only with all his pockets and both hands full.

Some believed that Hudson was like Hudson because nobody cared enough for him to try to improve him.

He was nobody's fool. But apart from making that clear there was really no other term to use on him. He was a Nero with wet matches, and like Nero he was one for the auguries. If you could persuade him that the tie and the waistcoat he was wearing were a lucky combination of colours, he would stand you a drink or give you a job. Then he would pump you till you admitted it was only lucky on days of the full moon and half-day closing.

He had made money and married into quality. Though it remained a mystery to everyone including himself how he got invited to the home of Fetterton's long-sitting Member of Parliament, Sir Stamford Raffles, Hudson did. He entered. He wooed and won Angelica Madison Raffles.

Like Miranda in *The Tempest* or that benighted creature in one of Purcell's operas, Angelica gobbled down the first man planted in her way, and got such bad indigestion that she died shortly afterwards. So did Stamford Raffles, leaving Hudson (for want of time to dash off a preventative will) the finest house in the region, Horbury Place.

A ruthless ability to take advantage of any lucrative situation had made Hudson cock of the walk. Now he was lord of the manor and he was quick to realize how his public esteem and private confidence could be elevated to new heights.

The answer lay in public service.

He got himself on to the council. He confounded the tradition of English law by becoming a Justice of the Peace – on demand. He began to do good works. Overnight, he became cultural. He quite rightly crushed one cinema in the town which showed dirty foreign films and brought people into active and intelligent participation with Splash Bingo, a new version of the game where on the winning call, a pretty girl in a bathing costume tumbled into illuminated water.

He encouraged sport by building a first class greyhound stadium on the local athletic track, and rescued the Town Hall from a touring orchestra (which only weirdies and beardies went to anyway), for exciting weekly tournaments of professional wrestling.

After all, who bought Hudson's cakes, hot-dogs and confectionary at athletic tracks where they didn't have two spectators to rub together; or who crunched Hudson's candy rock in the middle of Palestrina?

Indeed, as Billy Hudson was always fond of saying when his contributions to the leisure-time of Fetterton's citizens was brought up, 'Who the hell wants to listen to Minestroni anyway?'

James Watson

15
Everyday life

A group of five readings to be used as occasion demands.

1: EMBARRASSING MOMENTS

The college dining hall was a gloomy, oak-panelled place, and fifteen students ate at each of the tables. For some meals there was what was called 'Family Service'. This meant that – turn and turn about – two or three of the students were responsible for carrying the food from the servery to the table.

One lunchtime, a particular student was carrying a pile of fifteen plates, and balanced on top of them, a metal dish of boiled tinned tomatoes. He was in a hurry to reach the table: perhaps the plates were hot: and perhaps it was dropped butter or spilt grease on the floor. . . .

He made a wild, desperate attempt to steady himself, gained his balance for a moment, lost it again, staggered, tottered – the dish fell, then most of the plates.

For a moment, all over the dining hall, there was silence. Then loud, loud, lusty, ironic cheers – and the loudest were from his table, from his friends.

Broken white heavy institution plates – far more than fifteen there seemed; the juice of the tomatoes; and the tomatoes them-selves – they spread for yards down the central aisle of that dining hall. People began to step aside to avoid the sticky mess, a traffic jam built up – and as the poor student made off, looking for a mop and pail, he was offered wit and advice, but not help.

How everyone loved that moment! It was worth being without tomatoes, just for the entertainment.

He didn't hurt himself, physically. But despite its being an accident, something that could have happened to anyone, he suffered terrible embarrassment. Red, hot, acute embarrassment.

An even worse kind of embarrassment is the kind that is caused deliberately; when we actually set out to embarrass a person in order to raise a laugh from everyone else. And the remark may be made by a teacher who wants to make sure the whole class laughs at a silly mistake, and wants to use that mocking laughter to make sure the mistake won't happen again; or it may be made by a parent who tells other adults about the 'childish' habit their son has got – sucking his thumb, chewing his nails, or whatever – in the hope that they will embarrass him out of the habit. Or it may be made by a so-called friend, who is seeking popularity with the rest of the class.

Most of us have experienced the agony of being embarrassed, either accidentally or deliberately. Accidents can't always be avoided, but before we ever make a deliberately embarrassing remark, we should perhaps remember these lines by a thirteen year old:

> 'My friends' laugh and jeer at me,
> People I once trusted
> Mock me and scoff at me.
> 'Idiot, nit, thicky' they cry
> And it echoes around my head.
> I feel small and embarrassed
> As if the world was fighting me
> And I was losing.

David Self

2: IN THE FASHION

I think the first time I realized there was such a thing as fashion was when I was about eleven. I had just started high school and although I'd made some friends there I had never met them out of school until they asked me to go to a dance at the Mecca with them one Saturday afternoon. I had never been to a dance before and I set off feeling very excited. I had my best dress on, pink taffeta with satin ribbons threaded through it. My Mum thought I looked lovely. Nobody would have a dress as pretty as mine on. When I got there nobody did. They were all wearing skirts or jeans and polo-necked jumpers. I didn't take my coat off all afternoon. I would have looked like a Christmas tree fairy.

Fashion then was simply a matter of looking as much like everybody else as possible. A few years later, round about fifteen or sixteen, it was exactly the opposite. The ideal then was to dress and make-up as outrageously as you dared so that people would look at you, preferably boys.

I remember my sister saying that she wouldn't be seen dead with a boy whose trouser bottoms were wider than fourteen inches. She was a teenager at the start of rock and roll and her boyfriends fell into two categories. The first was the out and out Teddy boy with drape jacket, drainpipe trousers and bootlace tie. The other type wore a black leather jerkin with studs in, an open-necked shirt with the collar turned up, tight jeans and rode a 500 cc. Norton. Both sorts plastered their hair with Brylcreem and combed it into a high quiff off the forehead and a 'd.a.' at the back, with long curly sideboards. Dad wouldn't have any of them in the house, but she got engaged to one of the rockers and eventually married him. Mum and Dad forecast absolute disaster but now he drives a Mini, wears nothing trendier than a grey suit and works in the Town Hall. All of which seems a bit of a disaster to me, but it depends which way you look at it I suppose.

I think the best thing about today's fashion is that there aren't any fixed rules. You no longer have to torture yourself in order to be in fashion like people did up to a few years ago. Now you can wear just about anything that suits you and it will be fashionable. All you have to do is cover up your bad points and show off your good ones. Mind you, I'm still trying to decide what my good point is so that I can emphasize it.

Lesley Davies

3: HAPPINESS

Everyone wants to be happy; that is an indisputed fact. Yet because happiness is such a personal thing and can mean different things to people, it is difficult to define, capture and keep.

Here are eight suggestions as to how happiness can be achieved.

1   Do not waste your valuable time by worrying over things over which you have no control. This is negative thinking, causing you loss of sleep and stealing your peace of mind.

2   Work creatively and with imagination towards improving

your life and circumstances. Imagination is far more effective than strength of will and if you imagine yourself as successful and happy you will become so. Try it and see!

3 Learn to enjoy your relationships with others without feeling that they are vital to your happiness. Do not make demands on them that they find difficult to fulfil. Be prepared to give more to a relationship than you take out, and always be a little kinder than necessary.

4 Try to avoid gloomy people and depressing discussions. Always be ready to listen sympathetically and give helpful advice, but do not be drawn into general gossip about the terrible state of the world and the wickedness of people. This is not being selfish, just realistic.

5 Look for reasons for pleasure and satisfaction in your life; they are always there, and are much better dwelt on than the things that have gone wrong. Happiness, like depression, is self-generating. Believe you are content, and you have more chance than ever of achieving contentment than if you constantly grumble and fret about what is less than perfect about your life.

6 Start each day by deciding that you are going to be happy and successful. Remember that each day is a fresh start, and the beginning of the rest of your life! Sobering thought!

7 End each day by consciously 'wrapping up and setting aside' problems which you cannot improve or solve. Dwelling on these worries only achieves your own depression.

8 Remember that the happiest people ask the least from life. Their reasons for happiness and peace of mind come from within themselves and they have created their own peaceful world, based on self-knowledge and total self-acceptance which is quite independent of other people and circumstances.

Heather Causnett

4: MANNERS

Two views on manners:

(a) 'Take your elbows off the table,' I heard a mother say in a café the other day. 'Why?' said her child, as I guessed it would. 'Because it's rude,' said his mother, as I was absolutely certain she would.

The only answer in our house was a sharp rap from an extending toasting fork that my mother kept hanging on the back of her chair, ever ready to deal with an offence against table manners. Some of the things that gave offence seemed reasonable enough, like several hands fighting over the same fancy cake, playing tunes with your fork on your cup, constructing irrigation systems out of mashed potatoes and gravy, or igloos out of tinned half pears or even, I suppose talking with your mouth full.

But some others seemed arbitrary and unexplicable. Worse even than putting your elbows on the table was holding up knife and fork vertically in your fists, as you had seen people do in old cartoons or illustrations in Dickens. This, I now suppose, was banned because it smacked of shameless gluttony. To take the last piece of anything off a plate – the last slice of bread, the last scone, was another breach of manners. This rule was absolute and inflexible when we were very young, and the plates were taken back to the kitchen and the last biscuit or cake put back in the tin. But as we grew older– or perhaps richer– you could ask if anyone else wanted the last one and have it yourself if they didn't. (The trick here, of course, was to be the first one to ask.)

Harry Whewell

(b) The first and great characteristic of what is called good-breeding is perfect ease of manner and the absence of all fussiness. Whatever the company we may be thrown into, whatever the circumstances, this quiet ease should never be allowed to forsake us, in our endeavours to be polite, we must be careful not to run into any extremes, but bear in mind that good manners show themselves where to the vulgar eye they are the least observable.

How much more difficult is it than people suppose to shake hands well! In what a variety of ways are our hands shaken in the course of the year, and how few of those ways are pleasant ones! Sometimes our hands are seized and violently agitated to and fro. At others, a limp, nerveless something is dropped into our outstretched palm, which shows no sign of life while in our possession. And there are people who, from no feeling of affection, but simply from a vicious habit intended to express heartiness and cordiality, squeeze your fingers until the rings upon them enter into your flesh. Others – and I think this the most trying ordeal – retain your hand in theirs for a length of time, and ever and anon give it a little shake. No, each of these forms of hand-shaking is most irritating and objectionable. Take the hand offered you firmly, be careful to grasp the hand not the fingers merely, which has a ridiculous effect, give it a gentle pressure and then relinquish it, do not lift up to shake, neither let it drop suddenly – heartiness and cordiality should be expressed without the slightest approach to boisterousness.

Lady Colin Campbell

Pupils might add to this assembly by sharing their own experiences and views on the subject of manners (for example, on buses, at dances, etc.). A conclusion might be for a pupil to interview an adult who cares about good manners on this subject.

5: WHAT TO DO EACH MORNING AND EACH NIGHT

The following advice was published in 1543, in a book called A Dietary of Health.

In the morning:
When you be out of your bed, stretch forth your legs and arms and your body, cough and spit. After you have evacuated your body, comb your head oft, and so do divers times in the day. And wash your hands and wrists, your face and eyes and teeth, with cold water; and after that you be apparelled, walk in your garden or park, a thousand pace or two. And then great and noble men do use to hear mass, and other men that cannot do so, but must apply their business, doth serve God with some prayers, surrendering thanks to him for his manifold goodness, with asking mercy for their offences. And before you go to your refection, moderately exercise your body with some labour, or playing at the tennis, or casting a bowl, or poising weights or plummets of lead in your hands, or some other thing, to open your pores, and to augment natural heat.

In the evening:
After that you have dined and supped, labour not by-and-by after, but make a pause, sitting or standing upright the space of an hour or more with some pastime: drink not much after dinner.

At your supper, use light meats of digestion, and refrain from gross meats; go not to bed with a full nor an empty stomach. And after your supper make a pause ere you go to bed; and go to bed, with mirth, or have merry company about you, so that to bedward no anger nor heaviness, sorrow nor pensivefulness, do trouble or disquiet you. To bedward and also in the morning, use to have a fire in your chamber, to waste and consume the evil vapours within the chamber, for the breath of man may putrefy the air within the chamber. When you be in your bed, lie a little while on your left side, and sleep on your right side.

Andrew Boorde

16
Tolerance

1: THE BUS DRIVER

This anecdote is taken from a play called The Kitchen. *The speaker is a chef called Paul.*

Next door to me, next door where I live is a bus driver. Comes from Hoxton; he's my age, married and got two kids. He says good morning to me; I ask him how he is; I give his children sweets. That's our relationship. Somehow he seems frightened to say too much, you know? God forbid I might ask him for something. So we made no demands on each other. Then one day the busmen go on strike. He's out for five weeks. Every morning I say to him: 'Keep going mate, you'll win'. Every morning I give him words of encouragement. I say I understand his cause. I've got to get up earlier to get to work but I don't mind. We're neighbours, we're workers together, he's pleased. I give him money for the strike fund. I can see he's pleased. Then one Sunday, there's a peace march. I don't believe they do much good but I go, because in this world a man's got to show he can still say his piece. The next morning he comes up to me and he says, now listen to this, he says. 'Did you go on that peace march yesterday?' So I says, yes, I did go on that peace march yesterday. So then he turns round to me and he says: 'You know what? A bomb should've been dropped on the lot of them! It's a pity,' he says, 'that they had children with them, 'cos a bomb should've been dropped on the lot!' And you know what was upsetting him? The march was holding up the traffic, the buses couldn't move so fast!

Now I don't want him to say I'm right, I don't want him to agree with what I did, but what makes me so sick with terror is that he didn't stop to think that this man helped me in my cause so maybe, only *maybe*, there's something in his cause, I'll talk about it. No! The buses were held up so drop a bomb, he says, on the lot! And you should've seen the hate in his eyes, as if I'd murdered his child. Like an animal he looked. And the horror is this – that there's a wall, a big wall between me and millions of people like him. And I think – where will it end? What do you do about it?

Arnold Wesker

2: 'THEM' AND 'US'

What is it that makes a human individual one of 'them', to be destroyed like a verminous pest, rather than one of 'us', to be defended like a dearly beloved brother? What is it that puts him into an out-group and keeps us in the in-group? How do we recognize 'them?

The different classes, the different occupations, the different age-groups, they all have their own characteristic ways of talking, dressing and behaving. Each sub-group develops its own accents or its own slang. The style of clothing also differs strikingly, and when hostilities break out between sub-groups, or are about to break out (a valuable clue), dressing habits become more aggressively and flamboyantly distinctive. In some ways they begin to resemble uniforms. In the event of a full-scale civil war, of course, they actually become uniforms, but even in lesser disputes the appearance of pseudo-military devices, such as arm-bands, badges and even crests and emblems, become a typical feature. In aggressive secret societies they proliferate.

These and other similar devices quickly serve to strengthen the sub-group identity and at the same time make it easier for other groups inside the tribe to recognize and lump together the individuals concerned as 'them'. But these are all temporary devices. The badges can be taken off when the trouble is over.

The badge-wearer can quickly blend back into the main population. Even the most violent animosities can subside and be forgotten. An entirely different situation exists, however, when a sub-group possesses distinctive *physical* characteristics. If it happens to exhibit, say dark skin or yellow skin, fuzzy hair or slant eyes, then these are badges that cannot be taken off, no matter how peaceful their owners. . . .

Rationally, the rest of the tribe knows perfectly well that these physical 'badges' have not been put there on purpose, but the

112

response is not a rational one. It is a deep-seated in-group reaction, and when pent-up aggression seeks a target, the physical badge-wearers are there, literally ready-made to take the scapegoat role.

A vicious circle soon develops. If the physical badge-wearers are treated, through no fault of their own, as a hostile sub-group, they will all too soon begin to behave like one. Let us illustrate what happens, using an imaginary example. These are the stages:

1 Look at that green-haired man hitting a child.
2 That green-haired man is vicious.
3 All green-haired men are vicious.
4 Green-haired men will attack anyone.
5 There's another green-haired man – hit him before he hits you.

(The green-haired man, who has done nothing to provoke aggression, hits back to defend himself.)

6 There you are – that proves it: green-haired men *are* vicious.
7 Hit all green-haired men.

This progression of violence is, of course, ridiculous, but this does not stop them becoming a reality.

After the green-haired men have been hit for no reason for long enough, they do, rather naturally, become vicious.

Desmond Morris

3: KEEP OPEN THE WINDOWS OF YOUR MIND

A certain Greenland Eskimo was taken on one of the American North Polar expeditions a number of years ago. Later, as a reward for faithful service, he was brought to New York City for a short visit. At all the miracles of sight and sound he was filled with a most amazed wonder. When he returned to his native village, he told stories of buildings that rose into the very face of the sky; of tram-cars, which he described as houses that moved along the trail, with people living in them as they moved; of mammoth bridges, artificial lights, and all the other, dazzling features of the city.

His people looked at him coldly and walked away. And forth-with throughout the whole village he was nicknamed Sagdluk, meaning The Liar, and this name he carried in shame to his grave. Long before his death his original name was entirely forgotten.

Some time later, another Eskimo named Mitek visited New York, where he saw many things for the first time and was impressed. Later, upon his return to Greenland, he recalled the tragedy of Sagdluk, and decided that it would not be wise to tell the truth. Instead, he would narrate stories that his people could grasp, and thus save his reputation.

So he told them how he maintained a kayak on the banks of a great river, the Hudson, and how, each morning, he paddled out hunting. Ducks, geese and seals were to be had a-plenty, and he enjoyed the visit immensely. . . . Mitek, in the eyes of his countrymen, is a very honest man. His neighbours treat him with rare respect.

The road of the teller of new truths has always been rocky. Socrates sipping the hemlock, Christ crucified, Stephen stoned, Bruno burned at the stake, Galileo terrified into denying his discoveries – for ever could one follow that bloody trail through the pages of history.

Too many of us resent the impact of new ideas and look with suspicion on whoever imparts them to us. If a new idea invades our den, we rise up snarling from our winter sleep.

The Eskimos, at least, had some excuse. Their simple minds were unable to visualize the startling pictures drawn by Sagdluk. But there is no adequate reason why the average man should ever close his mind to fresh 'slants' on life. That is isolationism in its most tragic form.

Merle Crowell

4: OUR LAND

In 1970, the Peabody Coal Company began stripping coal from 65,000 acres it had leased from the Navajo and Hopi tribes of American Indians. Company officials declared that this mining would not damage Indian lands and in fact would improve the lives of many Navajos and Hopis. In disagreement with this action a group of Hopi wrote the following letter to President Nixon:

Dear Mr President,

We, the true and traditional religious leaders, recognized as such by the Hopi People, maintain full authority over all land and life contained within the Western Hemisphere. We are granted our stewardship by virtue of our instruction as to the meaning of Nature, Peace, and Harmony as spoken to our People by Him, known to us as Massau'u, the Great Spirit, who long ago provided for us the sacred stone tablets which we preserve to this day. For many generations before the coming of the white man, for many generations before the coming of the Navajo, the Hopi People have lived in the sacred place known to you as the Southwest and known to us to be the spiritual center of our continent. Those of us of the Hopi Nation who have followed the path of the Great Spirit without compromise have a message which we are committed, through our prophecy, to convey to you.

The white man, through his insensitivity to the way of Nature, has desecrated the face of Mother Earth. The white man's advanced technological capacity has occurred as a result of his lack of regard for the spiritual path and for the way of all living things. The white man's desire for material possessions and power has blinded him to the pain he has caused Mother Earth by his quest for what he called natural resources. And the path of the Great Spirit has become difficult to see by almost all men, even by many Indians who have chosen instead to follow the path of the white man.

Today the sacred lands where the Hopi live are being desecrated by men who seek coal and water from our soil that they may create more power for the white man's cities. This must not be allowed to continue for if it does, Mother Nature will react in such a way that almost all men will suffer the end of life as they now know it. The Great Spirit said not to allow this to happen even as it was prophecied to our ancestors. The Great Spirit said not to take from the Earth – not to destroy living things. The Great Spirit, Massau'u, said that man was to live in Harmony and maintain a good clean land for all children to come. All Hopi People and other Indian Brothers, are standing on this religious principle and the Traditional Spiritual Unity Movement today is endeavouring to reawaken the spiritual nature in Indian people throughout this land. Your government has almost destroyed our basic religion which actually is a way of life for all our people in this land of the Great Spirit. We feel that to survive the coming Purification Day, we must return to the basic religious principles and to meet together on this basis as leaders of our people.

Today almost all the prophecies have come to pass. Great roads

like rivers pass across the landscape; man talks to man through
the cobwebs of telephone lines; man travels along the roads in the
sky in his airplanes; two great wars have been waged by those
bearing the swastika or the rising sun; man is tampering with the
Moon and the stars. Most have strayed from the path shown us
by the Great Spirit. For Massau'u alone is great enough to portray
the way back to Him.

It is said by the Great Spirit that if a gourd of ashes is dropped
upon the Earth, that many men will die and that the end of this
way of life is near at hand. We interpret this as the dropping of
atomic bombs on Hiroshima and Nagasaki. We do not want to see
this happen to any place or any nation again, but instead we
should turn all this energy for peaceful uses, not for war.

We, the religious leaders and rightful spokesman for the Hopi
Independent Nation, have been instructed by the Great Spirit to
express the invitation to the President of the United States and all
spiritual leaders everywhere to meet with us and discuss the
welfare of mankind so that Peace, Unity, and Brotherhood will
become part of all men everywhere.

> Sincerely,
> (signed) Thomas Banyacya, for
> Hopi Traditional Village Leaders:
> Mrs Mina Lansa, Oraibi Claude Kawangyawma,
> Shungopavy Starlie Lomayaktewa,
> Mushongnovi Dan Katchongva,
> Hotevilla

5: LETTER FROM PRISON

*When the famous black leader, Martin Luther King, was in prison in
Birmingham, Alabama in the early sixties, he wrote what became a
famous 'Letter from Prison'. It was addressed to the local clergy, some of
whom had been protesting at his activities.*

*This passage is addressed to those Whites who say to Blacks, 'Be
patient, you will get equal rights before long. Just wait.'*

I guess it is easy for those who never felt the stinging darts of
segregation to say, 'Wait'. But when you have seen vicious mobs
lynch your mothers and fathers at will and drown your sisters
and brothers at whim; when you have seen hate-filled policemen

curse, kick, brutalize and even kill your black brothers and sisters with impunity; when you see the vast majority of your twenty million Negro brothers smothering in an air-tight cage of poverty in the midst of an affluent society; when you suddenly find your tongue twisted and your speech stammering as you seek to explain to your six-year-old daughter why she can't go to the public amusement park that has just been advertized on television and see tears welling up in her little eyes when she is told that Funtown is closed to coloured children, and see the depressing clouds of inferiority begin to form in her little mental sky, and see her begin to distort her little personality by unconsciously developing a bitterness towards white people; when you have to concoct an answer for a five-year-old son asking in agonizing pathos: 'Daddy, why do white people treat coloured people so mean?', when you take a cross country drive and find it necessary to sleep night after night in the uncomfortable corners of your automobile because no motel will accept you; when you are humiliated day in and day out by nagging signs reading 'white' men and 'coloured': when your first name becomes 'nigger' and your middle name becomes 'boy' (however old you are) and your last name becomes 'John', and when your wife and mother are never given the respected title 'Mrs', and when you are harried by day and haunted by night by the fact that you are a Negro, living constantly at tip-toe stance, never quite knowing what to expect next, and plagued with inner fears and outer resentments; when you are forever fighting a degenerating sense of 'nobodiness'; – then you will understand why we find it difficult to wait. There comes a time when the cup of endurance runs over, and men are no longer willing to be plunged into an abyss of injustice where they experience the bleakness of corroding despair. I hope, Sirs, you can understand our legitimate and unavoidable impatience.

Martin Luther King

17
Love

━━●◆●━━

A series of passages about the various aspects of love and the differences between true love and the less than genuine.

1: THE CLICHÉ EXPERT ON LOVE

(A passage for two readers)

    Popular films and fiction present a particularly rosy view of love. This dialogue satirizes some of the commoner clichés.

Q. As an expert in the use of the cliché, are you prepared to testify here today regarding its application in topics of sex, love, matrimony, and so on?

A. I am.

Q. Very good. Now, first, what is love?

A. Love is blind.

Q. Good. What does love do?

A. Love makes the world go round.

Q. Whom does a young man fall in love with?

A. With the Only Girl in the World.

Q. Whom does a young woman fall in love with?

A. With the Only Boy in the World.

Q. When do they fall in love?

A. At first sight.

Q. How?

A. Madly.

Q. They are then said to be?

A. Victims of Cupid's darts.

Q. And he?

A. Whispers sweet nothings in her ear.

Q. Who loves a lover?

A. All the world loves a lover.

Q. Describe the Only Girl in the World?

A. Her eyes are like stars. Her teeth are like pearls. Her lips are ruby. Her cheek is damask, and her form divine.

Q. Haven't you forgotten something?

A. Eyes, teeth, lips, cheek, form – no, sir, I don't think so.

Q. Her hair?

A. Oh, certainly. How stupid of me. She has hair like spun gold.

Q. Now will you describe the Only Man?

A. He is a blond Viking, a he-man, and a square shooter who plays the game. There is something fine about him that rings true, and he has kept himself pure and clean so that when he meets the girl of his choice, the future mother of his children, he can look her in the eye.

Q. How?

A. Without flinching.

Q. Are all the Only Men blond Vikings?

A. Oh, no. Some of them are dark, handsome chaps who have sown their wild oats, but this type of Only Man tells the Only Girl frankly about his Past. She understands and forgives.

Q. And marries him?

A. And marries him.

Q. Why?

A. To reform him.

Q. Does she reform him?

A. Seldom.

Q. Seldom what?

A. Seldom, if ever.

Q. Now, when the Only Man falls in love, madly, with the Only Girl, what does he do?

A. He walks on air.

Q. Yes, I know, but what does he do? I mean, what is it he pops?

A. Oh, excuse me. The question, of course.

Q. Then what do they plight?

A. Their troth.

Q. What happens after that?

A. They get married.

Frank Sullivan

2: THE FIRST TIME

The first time that I took a girl out was when I was in form P.6 in my primary school. I was only ten at the time and she was in P.7. I had to strike fast as she would be leaving the following year!

I had been keeping my eye on her for some time, then one day I slipped her a note in the dining centre. She went back to her table and read it. She said 'O.K. but my small brother will have to come too.'

I nearly died and slaved away for a week and three days for a quid, and my pocket money made it one pound two and six-pence. The day finally came and I called for them. Altogether it cost me seven bob for fares alone. Then we were hardly off the train when the little blighter asked for ice-cream, then sweets, and a go on the merry-go-round. That all amounted to another seven and six.

We went and had a bag of fish and chips each and then went off to the Tonic Cinema.

We got inside and she insisted on sitting in the very front row. We had only been sitting down for a few minutes when the boy behind began crunching his potato crisps. Then he produced a huge hunk of chewing gum wrapped in toilet paper out of his pocket and started slurping over that. The film finally ended and when we went outside, it was pouring. We were soaked to the skin by the time we reached the station. We soon were puffing out of one station and into another. By the time we reached her house the rain was running out of us. Her mother came out and gave me a clout and forbade me to see her again. That was the end of our romance and I didn't even get a kiss out of it all!

Raymond Campbell

3: A LOVE AFFAIR

This passage tells the story of a love affair. The narrator is Ruth Burrows, who is now a nun. As a nun, she has of course had to give up sex and marriage.

In this excerpt from her autobiography, she looks back to when she was twelve. At that time she went around with a 'gang' of friends of both sexes.

At twelve years of age a newcomer joined our gang. Two years older than most of us, I found him different from the other boys.

What is more, he treated me quite differently. I suddenly realized that I was a girl, a young woman. The desire to excel in games, to beat the boys, died away. Andrew would treat me as if I were made of china, never bowling me out, helping me off a wall, always making me precede him through a gate. We were in love. Andy was my world. I felt that I could not live without him. He was in my thoughts night and day. When he was absent I lived for the moment of his coming and would stand on the bank where I could see the trams coming into the terminus, watching for his wiry figure to leap off the tram with a twist all his own, a run up the hill.

The gang accepted this love-match quite simply, except that they were annoyed when our games went awry because of his partiality for me. But nearly always we were on the same side and this was taken for granted. Unashamedly we would walk along, our arms around each other's neck, our playmates quite content for us to be a little way ahead or behind. Sometimes, tired with our play, we would throw ourselves on the grass to rest and he would lay his head on my chest or I would lay mine on his. I loved to feel his hard, boyish body, so different in feel from a girl's.

Once or twice we exchanged shy kisses. I never remember wanting to go off in secret to show or give more of our bodies to one another. There seemed no need to do so. Our love was certain, free, full of mutual respect. I knew I could trust him. The grown-ups smiled at us but I knew I had to keep Andrew away from my father who became increasingly intolerant of boys coming to the home. This innocent love affair died a natural death through separation. Just before I entered the convent to become a nun, I met him again with his fiancée.

Ruth Burrows

4: A MUSLIM WIFE

The journalist Polly Toynbee tells the story of Naiemah, an English woman who has become a Muslim and married one. Her conversion happened when she was working as a secretary in Cambridge and met a Muslim family and became interested in their religion.

She spent more and more time with Muslims and adopted the full traditional dress. 'I learned that a woman's voice should be kept at a low pitch, so as not to attract men. She should never giggle or laugh in the presence of men, and should wherever possible stay in seclusion with other women. She should always wear loose garments to hide the shape of her body so as not to attract men. She should keep her adornments, her body and her hair, for the eyes of her husband and no one else.'

I asked if this seemed a harsh restriction. 'No. Actually it's quite fun. It's not a restriction at all. I prefer this way of life. I don't have to keep up a show in front of people any more. Western women slop around the house in an old dress when they are indoors with their husbands, and dress beautifully only when they go out and are looked at by other men. I don't think that's right. Our husbands should always see us at our best.'

At gatherings with other women, where she met to talk and study the Koran, she was often asked if she wanted to get married. 'My husband was pointed out to me across a hall, but I didn't meet him,' she says. They were told about one another and through an agent, he proposed to her. She refused twice, but after prayer, she accepted, and she met him just once. He is an Egyptian research student in computer studies. 'You pray to Allah to make the right decision, and you know you will.'

She accepts without question that he is the Imam of the family, and submits to all his decisions. 'Men and women are completely equal, but men are a degree above women.' Her husband broke in here. 'There must always be one captain of a ship,' he said. 'Marriage is a ship.' He says men have greater responsibilities. At the Day of Judgement a man will be answerable for more responsibilities than his wife.

Polly Toynbee

5: MOTHER AND BABY

The hands that touch the child reveal everything to it: nervousness or calm, clumsiness or confidence, tenderness or violence.

The child knows if the hands are loving. Or if they are careless. Or worse, if they are rejecting.

In attentive and loving hands, a child abandons itself, opens out. In rigid and hostile hands, a child retreats into itself, blocks out the world.

So that before we even think of recreating the prenatal rhythms which once flowed around this small body, we must let our hands lie on it motionless.

Not hands that are inert, perfunctory, distracted.
But hands that are attentive, alive, alert, responsive to its slightest quiver.
Hands that are light. That neither command nor demand.
That are simply there.
Light . . . and heavy in the weight of tenderness. And of silence.
Whose hands should hold the child? The mother's of course, provided that these hands know everything we have been saying.
This cannot be taught, although it can be forgotten.
Many mothers briskly pat their babies! Or shake them, thinking that they're rocking and consoling them . . .
Many have still, lifeless, uncomprehending hands.
Many are so wrapped up in their own emotions that they are literally in danger of smothering their children.

However, in most cases the women who has delivered her baby naturally will have had to rediscover her own body and to control its ill-timed impulses. So she is ready to hold and touch her baby. Despite her excitement, she will not overwhelm her child.

When the newborn child is placed on her stomach, when she lays her hands on it, she will think: 'My problems are over. But not my baby's.'
The delivery is over, but the baby's awakening has just begun.
It is on the first step of a wild adventure; it is transfixed with fear.

Do not move. Do not add to the baby's panic.
Just be there. Without moving. Without getting impatient. Without expecting anything.

At this point, out of consideration for her child, out of real – not egocentric – love, a woman will simply place her hands on its body. And leave them there, unmoving. They must give a message not of excitement, agitation and emotion, but of calm and lightness, and of peace.

Frederic Leboyer

18
Death

---

*Today, in the western world, young people are often shielded from the
facts and practicalities of death. To them it is something that happens
only on television or on the cinema screen. This may result in a failure
to cope emotionally when someone they know dies unexpectedly and
in a tendency to undervalue life. It is hoped that these readings will
encourage thoughts about death that are neither 'frightening' nor
morbid.*

1: NO MAN'S LAND

This passage comes from a novel called The Freedom Tree *by James
Watson. It is set in the Spanish Civil War and it is about what happens to
two teenage boys, Will and Griff, when they go to Spain to fight against
the Fascists led by General Franco. At this point in the story it is night
time and they have got lost in No Man's Land between the two armies
and are trying to get back to their own trench.*

In the dark, north, south, east and west wore the same feature-
less mask. The stars were overclouded, and anyway neither Will
nor Griff could read the stars.

The thought of crawling into a trench and finding not their
friends but a scowling enemy, made Will stop. 'We need to take
our bearings.'

Instinctively, they crouched down and at the very same
moment the hill halfway up the sky burst into flame. An explosion raised the lid of darkness.

Smaller explosions burst on the heels of the first.

There was a second of silence before the entire battle-front
unleashed its armoury. Somehow the blackness made things
worse. Distance closed in. Between a machine-gun barrel and the

victim was sightlessness – no matter that in daylight you couldn't
see the bullets either.

Head down, smelling the bitter winter earth, hands clamped
over ears. A bullet smashed stone close by. Another ricocheted
off rocks to the left or right.

Will raised his eyes as the intensity of the gunfire wavered –
and got the very worst shock of his life. His gaze fell on another
face.

The enemy soldier lay belly down, pointing in the direction of
his own trenches as Will and Griff were pointing at theirs. He was
as terrified as Will – and as young: wan faced, pop-eyed, immov-
able as though his limbs had been driven into the ground with
wooden stakes.

If he was armed, there was no sign of it. At the sight of two of
the enemy, he rolled sideways like a rabbit springing from the
hand about to descend upon its neck.

Will said 'Please!' It was all he could think of: please – don't do
anything, don't shoot, don't run. But Griff cut words. This was
the closest bang, the closest bullet and it drowned Will's
anguished 'No, Griff!'

Too late. The bullet was straight. The enemy turned half in a
circle. His hand was raised as if to some invisible support, some
arm held out to him in the last flash of his living mind.

His pop-eyed face fell back before the rest of him.

'There was no need!'

' 'Im or us.'

'He'd no gun.'

'Beggar that!'

Will was across the body. 'If he's only wounded –'

'Forget 'im. 'E's dead.'

The young Spaniard lay as only the dead lie. Yet Will would not
let him go. Feebly, he bent over him, willing breath back into him.

'Sorry, sorry . . .'

He no longer heard the flying bullets. He did not care whether
they struck him. The pop eyes were in his head. He could see
nothing but them.

One life. Sixteen years of caring and loving and feeding, of
laughing and crying and running talking – turned, in a single
moment, to cold flesh.

James Watson

2: THE FUNERAL

In this country the dead are either buried or cremated. Most religious denominations have some form of funeral ceremony. There is no reason why a body cannot be buried or cremated without any form of religious ceremony. The British Humanist Society (or the National Secular Society) will arrange a non-religious ceremony, if requested.This passage describes what happens at a church burial service and at a cremation.

At a burial preceded by a church service, the coffin is taken into the church by the bearers and placed in front of the altar. The mourners normally follow the coffin. In some Anglican as well as most Roman Catholic churches, the coffin is taken into the church the previous evening, and remains there before the altar until the service. After the service, the bearers take the coffin from the church to the grave while the mourners follow, led there by a member of the graveyard or cemetery staff. If the service has been held elsewhere, or there is no service, the coffin is carried direct from the hearse to the grave.

At some more formal funerals there are pall bearers, who walk alongside the coffin but do not carry anything. Originally they were used to carry the pall, a heavy canopy which was held over the coffin. Nowadays a form of pall is sometimes laid on top of a coffin to cover it during the service.

The bearers lower the coffin into the grave, on webbing slings, while the words of committal are said. The mourners sometimes throw earth on to the coffin, but they usually do not stay to see the complete filling-in of the grave, which is done later by the cemetery or graveyard staff.

Before a cremation, the service either takes place in a church with the words of committal said at the crematorium chapel, or the whole service is held at the crematorium. The coffin is taken into the crematorium chapel, followed by the mourners, and laid on the catafalque. As the committal sentences are being said, the coffin passes out of sight, either by being moved mechanically through a door, or by a curtain being drawn across it.

If the ashes are not left to be scattered or buried at the crematorium, you can ask the undertaker to collect them and post or give them to you. Most undertakers offer a selection of urns or special boxes for you to put the ashes in. Or an undertaker will, for a fee, scatter the ashes for you in a suitable part of a park or garden.

Consumers' Association

3: THE VIEW FROM THE HEARSE

On the day of a funeral, the body of the dead person is often taken in a procession from their home to the churchyard or crematorium. The procession is led by the hearse (the car carrying the coffin), and then the relatives follow in other cars. Sometimes the vicar or priest travels in the procession. One vicar describes what he sees 'from the hearse'.

Fashions at funerals have changed – not only in clothing but in behaviour, attitudes and expense. The view from the front seat of a hearse tells that many people are pretending that they cannot see what is happening.

Time was when every possible respect was paid – perhaps too much, but that was at a time when death was more frequent, and mortal life was shorter. It was also for most people the only time they had a bit of money, a family gathering, a feast, and commanded local 'respect'. Nowadays the increase in life's length, and the fact that more people die in hospital or away from home, lead us to behave often as if death did not exist.

Friends either ignore the bereaved, or else the subject. Shoppers shove their wheeled baskets straight through family funerals leaving church. Cars hoot and thrust ruthlessly past or into a funeral cortege. Gentlemen seldom stand or remove their headwear when a funeral drives past – they seem to be embarrassed to be seen showing courtesy. The majority of adults prefer to try and slip by, pretending that they have not seen. The children, in funeral hours, are usually in school.

Those seated within the large interiors of black limousines are not always blinded by tears – they can see and they have feelings. It is extraordinary the help that comes from seeing even total strangers make signs of kindness and concern which lighten that journey.

It is distracting and distressing that so many of our conversations are interrupted by those who won't wait. Society demands instant attention. In those brief seconds as death and resurrection pass by, with sadness and hope, our sympathy would be more convincing if we could make time to give others the right of way.

John Mason

4: WHAT I HAVE LIVED FOR

Bertrand Russell (1872–1970) was a famous mathematician and philosopher, and also a pacifist. He wrote many books and was well-known for his logical approach to life.

In this passage from his Autobiography, *he looks back on his life.*

Three passions, simple but overwhelmingly strong, have governed my life: the longing for love, the search for knowledge, and unbearable pity for the suffering of mankind. These passions like great winds have blown me hither and thither in a wayward course over a deep ocean of anguish, reaching to the very verge of despair. I have sought love, first, because it brings ecstasy, ecstasy so great that I would often have sacrificed all the rest of life for a few hours of this joy. I have sought it next because it relieves loneliness, that terrible loneliness in which one shivering consciousness looks over the rim of the world into the cold unfathomable lifeless abyss. I have sought it finally, because in the union of love I have seen, in a mystic miniature, the prefiguring vision of the heaven that saints and poets have imagined. This is what I sought, and though it might seem too good for human life, that is what at last I have found.

With equal passion I have sought knowledge. I have wished to understand the hearts of men: I have wished to know why the stars shine: I have tried to apprehend the Pythagorean power by which number holds sway above the flux. A little of this but not much I have achieved.

Love and knowledge, so far as they were possible, led upward towards the heavens. But always pity brought me back to earth. Echoes of cries of pain have reverberated in my heart. Children in famine, victims tortured by oppressors. helpless old people a hated burden to their sons, and the whole world of loneliness, poverty, and pain, make a mockery of what human life should be. I long to alleviate the evil, but I cannot. And I do suffer.

This has been my life. I have found it worth living, and would gladly live it again, if the chance were offered me.

Bertrand Russell

5: GOING TO HEAVEN

This is part of a story by E.M. Forster called Mr Andrews.

The souls of the dead were ascending towards the Judgement Seat and the Gate of Heaven. . . .

Among them ascended the soul of a Mr Andrews who, after a beneficent and honourable life, had recently deceased at his house in town. He knew himself to be kind, upright and religious, and though he approached his trial with all humility, he could not be doubtful of its result. God was not now a jealous God. He would not deny salvation merely because it was expected. . . .

'The way is long,' said a voice, 'but by pleasant converse the way becomes shorter. Might I travel in your company?'

'Willingly,' said Mr Andrews. He held out his hand, and the two souls floated upwards together.

'I was slain fighting the infidel,' said the other exultantly, 'and I got straight to those joys of which the Prophet speaks.'

'Are you not a Christian?' asked Mr Andrews gravely.

'No, I am a Believer. But you are a Moslem, surely?'

'I am not,' said Mr Andrews. 'I am a Believer.'

The two souls floated upwards in silence, but did not release each other's hands. . . .

'Relate to me your career,' said the Turk at last.

'I was born of a decent middle-class family, and had my education at Winchester and Oxford. I thought of becoming a missionary, but was offered a post in the Board of Trade, which I accepted. At thirty-two I married, and had four children, two of whom have died. My wife survives me. If I had lived a little longer I should have been knighted.'

'Now I will relate my career. I was never sure of my father, and my mother does not signify. I grew up in the slums of Salonika. Then I joined a band and we plundered the villages of the infidel. I prospered and had three wives, all of whom survive me. Had I lived a little longer I should have had a band of my own.'

'A son of mine was killed travelling in Macedonia. Perhaps you killed him.'

'It is very possible.'

The two souls floated upward, hand in hand. Mr Andrews did not speak again, for he was filled with horror at the approaching tragedy. This man, so godless, so lawless, so cruel, so lustful, believed that he would be admitted into Heaven. And into what a heaven – a place full of the crude pleasures of a ruffian's life on earth! But Mr Andrews felt neither disgust nor moral indignation. He was only conscious of an immense pity, and his own virtues confronted him not at all. He longed to save the man whose hand he held more tightly, who, he thought, was now holding more tightly on to him. And when he reached the Gate of Heaven, instead of saying 'Can I enter?' as he had intended, he cried out, 'Cannot *he* enter?'

And at the same moment the Turk uttered the same cry. For the same spirit was working in each of them.

From the gateway a voice replied, 'Both can enter.'

E.M. Forster

19

Why suffering?

1: THE PROBLEMS OF SUFFERING

To many people the world appears a hostile and unfriendly place. All around there is much pain and suffering and often it is the innocent who seem to suffer the worst disasters and hardships. Does this suggest that 'no-one' is in control, that there is no divine being who cares for creation? Surely, the argument goes, if God existed and if He were all-powerful and if He loved his creatures, then He would not allow them to kill each other in world wars and would certainly not attack them with plagues and earthquakes and famine. Does the existence of pain and suffering therefore mean that there is no God? Or does it mean He is unloving and uncaring?

So often, these basic questions form an insurmountable barrier to religious belief. When considering possible answers it may be helpful to appreciate that there are three types of suffering, which can be illustrated in the following ways:

(a) *Suffering caused by man's inhumanity to man (resulting from greed, desire for power, cruelty, thoughtlessness, etc.)*

Take the case of Patrick whose mother was unable to face the scorn of her community when she had an illegitimate child. The whole thing came to light because of a small boy's love of fishing. Sitting by the burn catching tiddlers Thomas heard strange sounds coming from a nearby chicken-house, chicken noises, and yet they seemed unlike any chicken talk he'd ever heard.

When he mentioned this at home his father told him not to be stupid. Thomas was not to be put off and the next time he went fishing he went up to the hut and found that the sacking which covered its windows ended an inch from the sill, leaving an air vent. A finger poked through and Thomas put his own hand over it, almost like a sign of friendship. Then he ran home.

131

His father still refused to believe him, finding it quite an incredible story since the field belonged to one of the most respected women in the village, a widow with four grown children. But Thomas wouldn't give up and the next day he managed to pull away the sacking. What looked back at was recognizably the face of a child, but it was so horrifying with its ingrained dirt, waist-length matted hair and strange chicken-like talks, that Thomas was terrified. He ran, and this time his father did believe him.

When Patrick was finally discovered he was seven and a half years old. His parents were intelligent and he had appeared to be a normal healthy baby when he left the Nursing Home where he was born. He was fostered at once, the putative father paying the foster-mother. But, two years later, the payments ceased and he was returned to his mother, who hid him in the chicken-house. This was ten feet by six feet and fitted with wire racks from which the wire had been removed, leaving Patrick to perch on the wooden struts. He moved against these bars in a sort of see-saw movement, and hopped about in frog-like movements from the back of his legs to his forearms. His toe-nails grew so long that he constantly tripped over them and twenty-eight healed fractures were found in his legs and arms from his falls. Having lived so long in the dark his face was deathly pale, and his shin-bones were concave, presumably in part because of his diet which consisted of crusts and potatoes thrown in to him as it might be to pigs. The floor of the hut was blanketed with layers of chicken feathers, excreta and the remains of the food.

Anne Allen and Arthur Morton

(b) *Suffering caused by man's incompetence (such as his failure to perfect a drug, his failure to realize a river is prone to flood a particular valley or that a mountain is volcanic, or his carelessness in controlling inventions such as the motor car).*

In 1966, in the Welsh mining village of Aberfan, one October morning, a man-made tip of slurry and other waste material from a coal mine slid down the mountainside and buried the village primary school.

The final death toll was a hundred and sixteen children and twenty-eight adults. There was hardly a house in the village that did not suffer the loss of at least one relative. If only we had used our knowledge better, if only we had planned properly, that tip would never have been built directly above a village school.

(c) *Suffering which is 'natural' and apparently unavoidable (such as the typhoon, the famine that results from bad weather, the deformity which afflicts a child from birth, the accident that does not stem from human error or the illness which has no known causes).*

In wide areas of Ethiopia drought has created the worst conditions of starvation in living memory.

Ethiopian officials say half a million people in the Ogaden region are affected and at least 70,000 are destitute in fourteen emergency relief camps. Eyewitnesses speak of countless children in the last extremes of hunger and of people, young and old, who resemble living skeletons.

In the Ogaden – as across the frontier of Somalia – herds have been virtually wiped out in many areas. The commissioner said the losses amounted to four-fifths of the cattle, and over half the sheep and goats in Ogaden. Even the camels, which were best able to withstand the drought, suffered badly and thirty per cent were estimated to have died.

(The following four passages illustrate some reactions to the question, 'Why must men suffer?')

2: THE BUDDHIST ANSWER

Buddhism began in north India in the sixth century B.C. Its founder (real or legendary) was the Hindu prince, Siddhartha Gautama, known as the Buddha – 'the enlightened one'. His father tried to protect Siddhartha from the realities of life and from any knowledge of suffering, but one day the prince persuaded his father to let him travel through the countryside. Much distressed by what he saw, he became a wandering hermit. However he rejected the austere life of the ascetic and followed 'the middle way'. One day, in his search for the meaning of life, he came to a great bodhi tree:

I shall sit beneath this tree and though my flesh and bones should waste away and my life-blood dry, I shall not stir again until I have found the truth.

At daybreak, the truth was revealed to him and he became the Buddha, the fully liberated one, the enlightened one. He returned to his family and taught the Four Noble Truths and the

Eightfold Path or 'middle way' that leads to the end of selfishness and suffering:

When we're full of selfish wants we no longer know what the world is really like. Put aside your desires and when you've dropped those thoughts which bind you, you'll see things as they really are, and that is happiness and freedom.

Understand yourself and the people about you properly; think how you can be of use to the world; speak the truth; be straightforward in your actions; choose a job which isn't harmful to others; try hard to find out what life is really about; take care of everybody and everything you meet; look beneath the surface of life to the mysterious source of your own existence.

Buddhism teaches a way of liberation from suffering through ethics and discipline. The more a person follows these rules, the sooner he or she reaches Nirvana. 'God' plays no part in this religion or philosophy and the Buddha never claimed to be anything other than a man.

The Buddhist answer to suffering lies with man: he must radiate compassion and so become a saviour to those who suffer, as is shown by this parable:

Once upon a time there was a woman who had an only son. One day, in his youth, that son died; and in her distress, the mother went to Buddha. 'My son has died,' she said. 'My only son. Why should this be?'

'Go,' said the Buddha. 'Go and bring me a mustard seed from each house in your village where there has never been a death.'

So the woman went back to her village and asked at each house, but of course at every house there had been a death so she went again to the Buddha. 'I cannot bring you a mustard seed', she said. 'At every house where I asked, there has been a death.'

'So it is,' said the Buddha. 'We must all suffer and we are all part of each other.'

David Self

3: PROMETHEUS

This Greek myth is the story of the god Prometheus and what he did for man, and how (in return) he was 'crucified', bound to a rock in order that mankind might benefit.

(This myth has obvious similarities to the crucifixion story, but there are also important differences which could be explored in discussion. These centre of course on the nature of Zeus, who, according to Greek myth, was keen to keep mankind in a subservient role.)

Prometheus taught men how to build houses, how to plough the earth and sow corn, how to reap it when it had grown, how to thresh out the grains and grind them between flat stones. He showed them how to catch and tame the dog to guard their houses and go hunting with them; the horse to draw carts, and the ox to pull the plough.

But it was slow work, since fire, the greatest aid, was missing. Without it meat had to be eaten raw, and tools could be made only of stone; bread could not be baked, and houses could not be warmed in winter.

'I must give Fire to mankind, the last and greatest of gifts,' thought Prometheus, 'but if I do so, I shall incur the jealous anger of Zeus, for he has said man should not have this power.'

Even so, because Prometheus knew that the gift of fire would benefit mankind, he set out for Olympus, carrying with him the hollow stalk of a fennel plant, filled with a white pith which would burn steadily like a candle. As day drew to an end, the sun god, Helios drove up in his shining chariot, and Prometheus stretched out his fennel-stalk and touched the wheel. Then, with the stalk burning slowly, he hurried down the mountain and, in a valley, he heaped up a pile of wood and kindled it.

Next day he began to teach men the uses of Fire. He showed them how to cook meat and bake bread; how to make bronze and iron; how to hammer the hot metals, and all the other crafts of the smith and the metal-worker.

So mankind came into his true inheritance: cities grew up, and men practised all the arts and crafts for which Greece was soon to become famous.

But Zeus, as soon as he became aware that his command had been disobeyed and the gift which he withheld from mankind had been stolen and given to men, summoned Prometheus before him.

In a voice like thunder he commanded Prometheus to be bound to the great mountain of Caucasus on the eastern edge of the world.

'There you shall lie,' he cried in his cruel rage, 'for ever and ever as a punishment for your daring and disobedience. The snows of winter will freeze you, and the summer sun will burn you; and your fate shall be a warning to all who would disobey!'

Then the demons Might and Force chained Prometheus to the mountainside with fetters that he could not break.

Isaiah, chapter 53 is a poem describing the suffering of a mysterious figure called 'the servant of the Lord', a scapegoat that would suffer for mankind. (The origin of the idea of a scapegoat is described in Leviticus, *chapter 16, verses 20 and 21.) N.B. The idea of a suffering servant is therefore present in Greek mythology, Judaism and Christianity.*

4: THE STORY OF JOB

One of the most famous attempts to answer the question 'Why must men suffer?' is to be found in the Old Testament. It is the story of Job.

Narrator: Job worshipped God. He did no wrong. He helped the poor and sick and gave help to anyone who needed it. He was humble and faithful to God.

Then a series of catastrophes happened to Job. His oxen and camels were killed. His sheep were struck by lightning His sons and daughters were killed when the house they were in was struck by a whirlwind. But Job still trusted in God.

Job: I was born with nothing and I will die with nothing. The Lord gave and now he has taken away. Blessed be the name of the Lord.

Narrator: Job then became ill: his body was covered with sores, like boils. Still he said nothing against God.

Job: When God sends us something good, we welcome it. How can we complain when he sends us trouble?

Narrator: Three of this friends tried to comfort him as he suffered, but eventually in his continued suffering, Job cursed the day he was born.

Job: I wish I'd died in my mother's womb or died the moment I was born! Why did I live to suffer?

Narrator: So his friends offer possible answers. First, Eliphaz who believes that Job must have done wrong because only the wicked suffer, and that he must accept his punishment.

Eliphaz: I have seen people plough fields of evil and sow wickedness like seed – like a storm, God destroys them in his anger!

136

Happy is the person whom God corrects! Don't resent it when he rebukes you!

Narrator: The second friend, Bildad, believes God will put things right in the end, and Job must be patient.

Bildad: God never twists justice.

Your children must have sinned against God and so he punished them as they deserved. Turn and plead with God. If you are honest and pure, God will help you and all your wealth will be nothing compared with what God will give you. God will never abandon the faithful – he will let you laugh and shout again.

Narrator: Zophar's argument is that really Job deserves to suffer far more.

Zophar: You claim you are pure in the sight of God! How I wish God would answer you! God is punishing you far less than you deserve! God knows which men are worthless, he sees all their evil deeds!

Narrator: One thing the Book of Job never suggests, like some religions, is that everything will all be right in the next life.

So is acceptance of suffering the only answer? Can you think of another answer, or do you agree with Job?

Job: I know, Lord, that you are all-powerful; that you can do everything you want. Your will be done. Amen.

(N.B. Chapter 42, verses 7–17, *are thought to be a later addition to the* Book of Job*).*

5: MY LIFE AND THOUGHTS

Albert Schweitzer (1875–1965) was a successful and famous German musician and philosopher who gave up a promising career to qualify as a doctor and then to go to equatorial Africa to found a leprosy hospital.

This is a short excerpt from his autobiography, in which he looks back on his life.

Only at quite rare moments have I felt really glad to be alive. I could not but feel with a sympathy, full of regret all the pain I saw around me, not only that of men but that of the whole creation. From this community of suffering I have never tried to withdraw myself. It seemed to me a matter of course that we should all take our share of the burden of pain which lies upon the world. Even when I was a boy at school it was clear to me that no explanation of the evil in the world would ever satisfy me, all explanations, I felt, at bottom had no other object than to make it possible for men to share in the misery around them with less keen feelings. That a thinker could reach the miserable conclusion that though this world is, indeed, not good, it is the best that was possible, I have never been able to understand.

But however much concerned I was at the problem of misery in the world, I never let myself get lost in brooding over it. I always have held firmly to the thought that each of us can do a little to bring some portion of it to an end. Thus I came gradually to rest content in the knowledge that there is only one thing we can understand about the problem, and that is that each of us has to go his own way, but as one who means to help to bring about deliverance.

Albert Schweitzer

20
Different faiths

1: HINDUISM

One of the main religions of India is Hinduism. Not all Indians are Hindus, not all Hindus live in India, but the two are very closely connected. Hinduism is very old; it's not so much one religion as many – and Hindus don't all believe the same things. Nevertheless, one thing most Hindus believe is that, after death, the soul is reborn in another form of life. If the person has been very good, then his soul goes straight to God. If however, he has performed any sinful actions, then his soul goes into another living being on earth. If he has been a very sinful person in the past then he is reborn as an animal.

If on the other hand, it has only been a moderately sinful action, then he'll be reborn as a human being, but at a humbler level in life.

This belief is expressed poetically in the Hindu scriptures, the Upanishads:

When the body falls into weakness on account of old age or disease, just as a mango-fruit is loosened from its stem, so the Spirit of man is loosened from the human body and returns by the same way to Life, wherefrom he came . . .

Even as a caterpillar, when coming to the end of a blade of grass, reaches out to another blade of grass and draws itself over to it; in the same way the Soul, leaving the body and unwisdom behind, reaches out to another body and draws itself over to it.

This cycle of birth, life, death and then rebirth is known as 'samsara'. For Hindus, this chance to 'have another go' at life is very attractive, for of course, the better we do in one life, so we shall be better off in the next.

'Even as a worker in gold, taking an old ornament, moulds it into a form newer and fairer, even so the Soul, leaving the body and unwisdom behind, goes into a form newer and fairer.'

Because of these beliefs, death is not regarded by Hindus as it is by many Westerners. For the Hindu, death is even something to look forward to, because it's a step towards a new life.

The ultimate aim of the Hindu is to move through a series of lives until you are with the gods. Hindu legend has it that one god, Vishnu, came to Earth as a man, Krishna; and in a holy book, the *Bhagavad Gita*, Krishna encourages his followers to leave all things behind, even life, in order to find salvation.

'Give thy mind to me, and give me thy heart, and thy sacrifice, and thy adoration. Leave all things behind, and come to me for thy salvation. I will make thee free and thou shalt fear no more.'

David Self

2: HAPPY HUNTING GROUNDS

William W. Warren was born in May 1825, the son of an American Indian mother who was a member of the Ojibway tribe, and a white father. His ancestry revealed that he was a descendant of Richard Warren, one of the 'Mayflower' pilgrims who landed in Plymouth in 1620. As a child he was schooled in the Indian manner, in 1842 he married and moved to what is now Minnesota, where he was employed as a government interpreter.

Fascinated by the traditions and tales of the 'old men', he spent hours visiting them in remote places. Warren died at the early age of twenty-eight just having completed a history of his nation, based upon Ojibway traditions and oral statements. The following passage describes the 'happy hunting grounds' of his people.

When an Ojibway dies, his body is placed in a grave, generally in a sitting posture, facing the west. With the body are buried all the articles needed in life for a journey. If a man, his gun, blanket, kettle, fire steel, flint and moccasins; if a woman, her moccasins, axe, portage collar, blanket and kettle. The soul is supposed to start immediately after the death of the body, on a deep beaten path, which leads westwards; the first object he comes to, in following this path, is the great Ode-e-min (Heart berry), or strawberry, which stands on the roadside like a huge rock, and from which he takes a handful and eats on his way. He travels on till he reaches a deep, rapid stream of water, over which lies the much dreaded Ko-go-gaup-o-gun, or rolling and sinking bridge; once safely over this as the traveller looks back it assumes the shape of a huge serpent swimming, twisting and untwisting its folds across the stream.

After camping out four nights, and travelling each day through a prairie country, the soul arrives in the land of spirits, where he finds his relatives accumulated since mankind was first created; all is rejoicing, singing and dancing; they live in a beautiful country interspersed with clear lakes and streams, forests and prairies, and abounding in fruit and game to repletion – in a word, abounding in all that the red man most covets in this life, and which conduces most to his happiness. It is that kind of paradise which he only by his manner of life on this earth, is fitted to enjoy.

William W. Warren

3: ISLAM

Islam stems from Christianity, and recognizes both Old and New Testaments and reveres all the biblical prophets. But it insists that Mohammed was the last and greatest prophet.

Mohammed was born in A.D. 570 in Mecca, then the religious centre for Arab idolatry; and his tribe, the Koreish, were the ruling bedouin. He married a wealthy widow called Khadija, and they had a daughter called Fatima, through whom all his descendants trace their line.

The first vision came to Mohammed when he revealed that the Archangel Gabriel commanded him 'Recite': he did so, and the words he spoke were the beginnings of the sacred book of the Koran, the basis of the law of Islam, teaching of the existence of Allah as the only God, and promising after-life.

He became convinced that he was the prophet of Allah. The Meccan merchants, outraged by his denunciations of the idols that attracted the pilgrim trade, threatened his life, and he fled to Yathrib in the north – later named Medina (City of the Prophet). The year of the Hegira, or flight, is the start of the Muslim calendar. Mohammed became the religious leader and governor of the city, and when war broke out between his followers and Meccans the fighting ended with his return to Mecca.

141

Mohammed did not institute an organized priesthood, but the Koran proclaimed a number of observances, the Five Pillars of Islam, which every believer must obey.

1 Belief in one god: 'There is no god but Allah; Mohammed is the Messenger of Allah.'
2 Prayer five times daily, facing Mecca.
3 Payment of the legal alms to the needy – two and a half per cent of the total yearly wealth of the donor.
4 Fasting from sunrise to sunset each day during Ramadan – traditionally the month in which the Koran was sent down for the guidance of the people.
5 Pilgrimage at least once in a lifetime to Mecca, money and health permitting.

Besides these main edicts, there are rules for daily life: pork and liquor are forbidden, as are gambling and money-lending.

The prophet died at the age of sixty-two at Medina in June, A.D. 632, and his followers were divided over the question of the succession. Those who had accompanied Mohammed in his flight from Mecca considered that Abu Bekr, the first Caliph, or Successor to Mohammed, was rightfully chosen. They and their descendants formed the majority group of Islam, the orthodox Sunni. Later, there was a dispute in succession between Ali, son-in-law of the prophet, and Osman, the third Caliph, and this was reflected in later centuries when the followers of Ali formed the more liberal Shi'ite sect.

The Observer

Most diaries indicate which year it is in the Muslim calendar, together with the date of the Islamic New Year. This information is often under the heading 'Common Notes'.

4: THE BIRTH OF THE SIKH RELIGION

Probably the most instantly recognizable member of a religion in Britain today is a male Sikh. His is almost invariably of Indian origin, he wears a beard and has his hair long bound up under a turban. He has a steel bracelet on his wrist: his surname is Singh.

The Sikhs form the newest of major world religions and they are fiercely monotheistic; that is, they believe that there is only one true God, who is invisible and all-powerful. Their God is, in essentials, the same God as that worshipped by Jews, Christians and Muslims and, humanly speaking, they came to the knowledge of that God through Muslim influence. Sikhism is, in fact, a kind of compromise between Islam and Hinduism, though it arose not through a desire for unity but through a prophet, or guru, Nanak, who lived from 1469 to 1538.

As a young man Nanak worked as a clerk in a Government office in Sultanapore in north-west India. He was a Hindu poet and, with his friend the minstrel Mardana, he composed and sang hymns to God.

He had already gathered a small band of disciples when he felt that he underwent a decisive experience. He had a vision in which he was taken into the presence of God and God gave him nectar to drink. God instructed him to go back into the world and spread true knowledge. Nanak thereupon composed the basic Sikh prayer, and this prayer is still recited daily by the devout.

'There is but one God whose name is True, the Creator, devoid of fear and enmity, immortal, unborn, self-existent, great and bountiful . . .'

Nanak, accompanied by Mardana, spent the rest of his life preaching God, the True Name: he did so mostly by singing his hymns. These hymns were later collected together into a single sacred volume, the Guru Granth Sahib, which holds a respected place in every Sikh temple (or Gurdwara). As Nanak sang, a man should crave for knowledge of God as he craves for food.

Colin Cross

Men, women and children, heads covered and wearing no shoes, approach the Guru Granth Sahib *on entering the Gurdwara. They prostrate themselves before it, making an offering of money or food.*

A Sikh may visit the Gurdwara at any time, especially in the early morning or the evening before or after the day's work. There is no 'sabbath' such as Jews, Muslims or Christians observe, though in Britain most gatherings are held on Sunday.

Some of the Sikh festivals observed in Britain and their approximate dates are:

The Birthday of   Late December or early January
Guru Gobind Singh

Hola Mohalla (Holi)*	Late February
Baisakhi*	April
Diwali* (see page 164)	Late October/early November
Birthday of Guru Nanak	Late November

* These are also Hindu festivals.

5: RASTAFARIANISM

For thousands of Jamaicans living in England repatriations means only one thing; a 'return' to Africa, and specifically to the 'promised land' of Ethiopia. This is the vision of the Rastafarians, who embrace the late Haile Selassie of Ethiopia as the living God and the returned Messiah.

The Rastafari movement, bred in the ghetto of Kingston, Jamaica, has taken hold – either as a religion, or a style of black consciousness – of the imagination of Jamaica's youth, and has spread to the streets of London, Birmingham and Manchester. Its followers are increasingly visible, their striped woollen 'tams' in the Rastafari colours covering their 'dread-locks'. Today it is the most powerful cultural force among young Jamaicans, and among the black youth of Britain, and its message is not race war, but peace, non-violence and an end to 'captivity' in the West.

At a point along the road between Kingston and Spanish Town, we turn off on to the dirt and towards the sea. In an open space, somewhere in this odd landscape, which is both dense, tropical hill country and the outer reaches of suburbia, the Twelve Tribes of Israel, one of the largest groups of Rastafarians in Jamaica, are holding a nocturnal meeting. It is already 11 p.m. but still about 75°F.

From the edges, the meeting of the Twelve Tribes presents an extraordinary sight. Under a high hill, with fires blazing in caves to keep the mosquitoes down, groups of Rastas are lit up in front of tall, pale green cacti. In the centre there is a circle of perhaps 2000 brethren, each with a woollen tam hiding his locks, knitted in the Rastafari colours.

These are *red*, for the blood of the martyrs, *gold* for Jamaica, *black*, for the colour of the Africans – Rastas do not consider themselves Jamaicans – and *green* for the sacred ganja herb, marijuana, and the green fields of Ethiopia, which is the promised land, and where they demand to be repatriated, 'under our own vine and fig tree.'

Brother Gad, a prophet, greeted us with consummate politeness and the authority and nobility common to many of the brethren. The cockerels and turtle doves in the compound drowned out our dialogue. He showed us goats and rabbits: 'I try to raise the things that God told us to name.'

Between the religious meetings, to keep the 'yout' (young people) out of harm's way, Gad organizes cricket and football matches. Twenty-two dreadlocks on the pitch below Dread Heights, in green, red and gold track suits, is an awesome sight. The reggae song says, with reason, 'Dread flash him locks anna weak heart drop'.

'Our motive,' said Gad, 'is to fulfil the people's wish to be repatriated to Ethiopia. Deep now in my mind I see that the time is going to come that you are going to have a mass movement of people to the land of Africa – not specifically Ethiopia.' Some of the Rastas see repatriation as a divine act. Gad and the Twelve Tribes, however, have already settled twenty-eight people on the five hundred acres of land given by Selassie in the fifties to descendants of African slaves in the West.

The Rasta movement was born in the ghetto in the fifties out of unemployment and despair. Gad himself was driven out when the movement suffered its worst persecutions under Jamaica's first Prime Minister after independence, Alexander Bustamante. He portrayed them as criminals and lunatics and his bulldozers flattened their bases in Trench Town and Back O'Wall in the mid-sixties, scattering them all over the island.

Since then the Rastas have gained some respectability if only because theirs is clearly the most powerful, indeed the only, cultural force on the island. Its styles and attitudes, if not its strict doctrines, have captured the hearts and minds of Jamaican youth (fifty-three per cent of the population is under nineteen). Its influence reaches from the ghetto, where it serves also as a disguise for criminals ('wolves in sheep's clothing'), to the middle class, where it is high fashion. The whole reggae music industry is bound up with it and acts as its communication system, projecting it worldwide.

It is hardly a nationalistic force, however. Common to the 100,000 or so true believers – who are loosely associated in various sects – is the belief that Jamaica is a hell on earth – the symbol of captivity for the black man, and of the slavedriver's whip – which the ultraconscious Rastamen say they can physically feel.

They have embarked, in Rastafarianism, on a mass psychoanalysis to find the black man's true identity, delving into the Bible, weeding out the parts introduced by the white man to conceal the true, black identity of 'the children of Israel.'

James Fox

SEASONAL
READINGS

The
Jewish New Year

In the Western calendar, the date of this festival varies from year to year, but is within the month of September. Its precise date can be found in most diaries.

The three pilgrim festivals celebrate particular events in Israel's national history. At New Year the emphasis is laid more on the individual. In Christian countries the New Year is not primarily a religious festival, but provides an excuse for lighthearted celebration. In contrast, the Jewish New Year is a solemn – though certainly not a miserable – occasion. It is the time when each man, woman and child pauses to remember the sins which he has committed during the past year.

The New Year is greeted quietly and soberly. Everyone eats an apple dipped in honey and wishes each other a sweet and happy New Year. In the synagogue a ram's horn is blown to mark the beginning of the ten days of repentance. The blowing of the horn brings many memories to the worshippers. It reminds them of the ram which was found in the thicket when Abraham was about to sacrifice Isaac. It reminds them of the horn that was blown as a warning when the Temple was about to fall. Most of all, it is a call to remind them of their sins. In the words of the prophet Amos, 'If a trumpet sounds the alarm, are not the people scared?' In the afternoon the people go to the bank of a river or to the seashore and throw crumbs out onto the water to symbolize their sins which will be separated from them. As they do so they quote the words of the prophet Micah, 'and you will cast all your sins into the depth of the sea'.

The days of repentance come to a close with the most solemn day in the Jewish calendar. At the time when the Temple stood in Jerusalem, the High Priest went alone into the holiest of holies, and there sprinkled the blood of a sacrificed animal. This act brought the people back to be *at one* with God. Hence it was called the Day of Atonement (Yom Kippur).

Sacrifices are no longer offered and there can be no priest to stand between the individual and his God. The individual therefore has to find his own repentance for the sins he had committed. Before Yom Kippur, Jews search their hearts so that they may become at one with God and their fellow men. No one can expect his sins to be forgiven unless he approaches Yom Kippur in a proper spirit. He must have put right any wrongs he may have done to his fellow man, and seriously mean to live in accordance with the law. In the words of the Mishnah:

If a man says, 'I will sin and repent, and sin again and repent', he will be given no chance to repent. If he says, 'I will sin and the Day of Atonement will effect atonement', then the Day of Atonement effects no atonement. For transgressions which are between man and God, the Day of Atonement effects atonement; but for transgressions that are between man and his fellow, the Day of Atonement effects atonement only if he has appeased his fellow.

Martin Ballard

Genesis, chapter 22, verses 1–14 *describes God's testing of Abraham*.

Harvest

1: THE CORN HARVEST

To grow and harvest grain is such a satisfying thing to do. It has a definite beginning and a definite ending. You sow the seed, you tend the plants carefully for perhaps nine months through all the stages of their growth and ripening, and finally you harvest your crop, and when this is done you feel some satisfaction.

Grain, especially wheat, is such a beautiful thing at every stage of its career. First the thin delicate spears of almost green appear through the brown earth; in due time these thicken out into a dark green carpet laid close to the ground; in the spring this mat of plants shoots upwards until in late May and early June the ears appear; and these gradually ripen into such a lovely golden brown that it seems a shame to reap them. But this must be done, and in doing it the farmer sets the seal on his year's work.

Everybody loves and respects the corn harvest. When we want to describe a plenteous supply of anything we use the expression 'Corn in Egypt' which is derived from the story of the famine in Genesis. It is this fear of famine which makes us all respect the grain crop, because we know that an acre of wheat will provide more human food than an acre of any other crop. Deep down in our minds we know that without the harvest of the earth we should all perish. Farming, even at this glut period of history, is still the foundation of life of the whole world. It is possible for a man and his family to live solely on the produce of a piece of land, but it is not possible for anyone to exist unless the land of the world is farmed. The farmer's produce runs the whole world. Without it, railways and ships would have nothing to carry, no factories would work, in fact without farming the whole fabric of world civilization would collapse.

Today, a great many people never come into contact with agricultural production at all, and the steady supply of commodities must appear to them sometimes as something of a miracle. In the back of their minds there is always the fear that this plenty, from which they help themselves, may one day cease to be.

A.G. Street

Christian Aid, Oxfam and War on Want all provide suggestions which can be developed at Assembly or in the classroom.

2: SUKKOT

The Jewish harvest festival is called the *Sukkot* or the Feast of Tabernacles. It follows the ceremony of *Yom Kippur*, the Day of Atonement, the holiest day of the year in the Jewish calendar. The Sukkot is an eight day festival. During this time the family take their meals in a temporary dwelling, a hut or booth roofed with leafy branches and decorated with flowers and fruit. It commemorates the shelter that God provided for His people three thousand years ago as they marched through the wilderness from Egypt to the promised land.

There are four special plants offered to God in the synagogue which symbolizes His care and continued presence, as well as man's own nature. These are the citron, the date palm, the myrtle, the willow, all of which grow abundantly in the Holy Land. The citron has taste and fragrance and is a symbol of those people who have intelligence and human kindness; the date palm has taste but not fragrance and symbolizes those who have intelligence but are not kind and neighbourly; the myrtle has a wonderful fragrance but not taste; it represents 'those whose kindness sweetens the atmosphere about us'; finally, the willow has no taste or smell – it is simply a part of God's creation. In the same way there are men and women in no way distinguished yet all are included in God's plan of love and care.

These plants are brought to the synagogue. During the reciting of the Psalms of Thanksgiving they are pointed in six directions – the four points of the compass and above and below.

Raymond Trudgian

3: ALL IS SAFELY GATHERED IN

From our seats in the choir we watched the year turn: Christmas, Easter and Whitsun, Rogation Sunday and prayers for rain, the Church following the plough very close. Harvest Festival was perhaps the one we liked best, the one that came nearest home. Then how heavily and abundantly was our small church loaded; the cream of the valley was used to decorate it. Everyone brought of his best from field and garden; and to enter the church on Harvest morning was like crawling head first into a horn of plenty, a bursting granary, a vegetable stall, a grotto of bright flowers. The normally bare walls sprouted leaves and fruit, the altar great stooks of wheat, and ornamental loaves as big as cartwheels stood parked by the communion rails. Bunches of grapes, from the Squire's own vines, hung blue from the lips of the pulpit. Gigantic and useless marrows abounded, leeks and onions festooned the pews, there were eggs and butter on the lectern shelves, the windows were heaped with apples, and the fat round pillars which divided the church were skirted with oats and barley.

Almost everyone in the congregation had some hand in these things. Square-rumped farmers and ploughmen in chokers, old gardeners and poultry-keepers, they nodded and pointed and prodded each other to draw attention to what they had brought. The Church was older than its one foundation, was as old as man's life on earth.

The seed of these fruits, and the seed of these men, still came from the same one bowl; confined to this valley and renewing itself here, it went back to the days of the Ice. Pride, placation, and the continuity of growth were what we had come to praise. And even where we sang, 'All is safely gathered in', knowing full well that some of Farmer Lusty's corn still lay rotting in the fields, the discrepancy didn't seem important.

Laurie Lee

Suitable Bible readings for Harvest include: Psalms 65 and 145; Luke chapter 12, verses 16–21; 2 Corinthians, chapter 2, verses 6–15.

United Nations Day
(24 October)

The United Nations Organization is an association of states pledged to maintain international peace and security, and to promote international co-operation.

It succeeded the League of Nations.

The UN Declaration of the Rights of the Child proclaims:

The Right to affection, love and understanding.

The Right to adequate nutrition and medical care.

The Right to free education.

The Right to full opportunity for play and recreation.

The Right to a name and nationality.

The Right to special care, if handicapped.

The Right to be among the first to receive relief in times of disaster.

The Right to learn to be a useful member of society and to develop individual abilities.

The Right to be brought up in a spirit of peace and universal brotherhood.

The Right to enjoy these regardless of race, colour, sex, religion, national or social origin.

Hallowe'en
(31 October)

Its origins lie in the old pagan fire festival of Samhain and it is the night when ghosts walk. Hallowe'en is on 31 October, the day before All Saints' Day. On this night the dead were believed to return to their old homes to warm themselves in front of the fire. It was also a witches' festival or sabbat.

The Witches' Sabbat was held at night, often in the open air and in some remote and lonely spot. It was a combination of religious ceremony, magical rite and secular business presided over by the Grand Master who represented the god – the 'Devil' of the trials. Masked, disguised and perhaps horned and enthroned in the middle of a ring of excited and adoring witches, he must have seemed an imposing figure against a background of darkness lit only by the flames of candles and torches.

Today we try to frighten ourselves with masks and turnip lanterns in memory of the witches and ghosts of old. There are a number of ancient traditions connected with Hallowe'en:

Pull a cabbage from the ground at midnight:
the size of it will denote the size of your future partner.

Put nuts side by side on the grate:
if they burn quietly, you will have a happy marriage;
if they explode and jump apart . . .

Sit with a mirror before you and another behind you, eating an apple and combing your hair; your future husband will appear behind you in the mirror.

Roast parsnips, nuts and apples on an open fire. When the fire is low, collect the ashes in a circle and around the circumference put a stone to represent everyone present; next morning, if any stone is displaced or injured, the person it represents will be dead before next Hallowe'en.

Make the ghosts of your ancestors as welcome as you can.

1 November is All Saints' Day when Christians celebrate and give thanks for the lives of all Christian saints, known and unknown. 2 November is All Souls' Day, a day of prayer for all those who have departed from this life.

Remembrance Sunday

A veteran soldier of World War I was discussing Remembrance Sunday with a young man. The young man, wishing to impress and please the elder said: 'Those soldiers gave their lives that we might live, we should remember that.'

The old fellow was angry. 'Rubbish,' he snapped. 'Nobody gave anything. It was taken away in the crudest possible manner. That is what we should never forget.'

How, though, did the poppy become the symbol of remembrance for those who lost their lives in war?

The Flanders Poppy was first described as the 'Flower of Remembrance' by Colonel John McCrae, who before the First World War was a Professor of Medicine in Montreal. At the outbreak of the First World War he became a Medical Officer with the first Canadian Army contingent, in France.

At the second battle of Ypres in 1915, when in charge of a small first-aid post and during a lull in the action, he wrote, in pencil, on a page torn from his despatch book, the following verses:

> In Flanders' fields the poppies blow
> Between the crosses, row on row,
> That mark our place: and in the sky
> The larks, still bravely singing, fly
> Scarce heard amid the guns below.
> We are the dead. Short days ago
> We lived, felt dawn, saw sunset glow,
> Loved and were loved, and now we lie
> > In Flanders' fields.
>
> Take up our quarrel with the foe;
> To you from failing hands we throw

The torch: be yours to hold it high.
If ye break faith with us who die
We shall not sleep, though poppies grow
In Flanders' fields.

The verses were published under the title 'In Flanders' Fields', in the magazine *Punch*.

In May 1918 Colonel McCrae was brought as a stretcher case to one of the big hospitals on the channel coast of France. On the third evening he was wheeled to the balcony of his room to look over the sea towards the cliffs of Dover. The verses were obviously in his mind, for he told the doctor who was in charge of his case:

'Tell them this,
If ye break faith with us who die, we shall not sleep.'

The same night Colonel McCrae died.

The First World War finally came to an end in November 1918, when an Armistice was declared, so that peace-terms could be arranged. At 11 a.m. on 11 November, the last shot of the War was fired. For many years afterwards Armistice Day was observed on the 11 November, but now it is known as Remembrance Sunday, and is held always on the second Sunday in November.

An American lady, Miss Moina Michael, had read the poem and was greatly impressed, particularly by the last verse. The wearing of a poppy appeared to her to be the way to remember those who had been killed in war.

Two days before Armistice was signed, Miss Michael was presented with a small gift of money by some of the overseas War Secretaries of the Y.M.C.A. for whom she worked. She told them she was going to buy twenty-five red poppies with the money. This she did: she wore one herself, and each Secretary there bought one from her. It is claimed, probably rightly, that this was the first group selling of poppies.

The French Secreatry, Madame Guerin, had a practical and useful idea. She visited various parts of the world to suggest that artificial poppies should be made and sold to help ex-Service men and their dependants in need.

As a result the first ever Poppy Day was held in Britain on 11 November 1921. The poppies were obtained from a French organization, which used its profits to help children in the War-devastated areas.

Earl Haig (who had been Commander-in-Chief in France) used to say that the provision of work for disabled ex-Servicemen was as important as raising money.

The poppies we wear today are made by disabled ex-Servicemen working in the Royal British Legion Poppy Factory Ltd in Richmond, Surrey. Over the years the factory has provided a livelihood for some 1500 people – a human war memorial, as it has been described.

Royal British Legion

In 1980 production figures at the Poppy Factory were as follows:

47,000,000 standard poppies
More than 70,000 wreaths
250,000 Remembrance Crosses
1,000,000 car poppies
Over 1,000,000 poppies of other types

The Poppy Appeal in 1980 raised nearly £5 million and was used (as it is each year) to help ex-Servicemen and their relatives.

Advent

The four weeks before Christmas are known by Christians as the season of Advent. Advent is a Latin word meaning 'the coming' and in Advent, Christians prepare for the coming of Jesus to earth.

This time of year is also a time for other preparations – in particular, putting up Christmas decorations.

The town's main street has of course been decorated for several weeks. From lamp-post to lamp-post there droop garlands of garish light bulbs, and crowning each post is an electric snow flake, flickering in the evening light.

The shop windows are decorated too, in two quite different styles.

In some, there are nativity scenes. Around a plastic manger, imitation fire-resistant straw engulfs a plastic Mary and her plastic baby. Overhead there blinks an electric star.

In other windows, there's the other god: a fat, old man. He wears red robes, black boots and long stage whiskers. He likes the rich: to them he gives most of his presents, like scent and big cigars, fattening sweets and drink. As you go into his shops, you'll hear loudspeakers broadcast his manic laugh. And he laughs with good reason. He has won. He has defeated now the Virgin and her child and with his sleigh full of unnecessary objects, he drives his animals across the sky. And this god's name is Father Christmas.

Father Christmas is a modern name for Santa Claus, whose name comes from St Nicholas, or Saint Nikolaus, the patron saint of children.

According to custom, and especially in France and Holland and Hungary, St Nikolaus was supposed to go round distributing presents to children on his saint's day, 6 December. Actually, he

was supposed to give presents only to those children who had
been good. Those who had not been good received a whipping!

The new Santa Claus, with his reindeer and white beard and
red robe, was invented in America about a hundred years ago.

Last century also saw the invention of the Christmas card – the
first one was sent in 1846; and ever since then, one of our Christmas traditions has been choosing and sending Christmas cards.

Another Christmas tradition is decorating the house, especially with holly. Christians say that the prickles and the red
berries of the holly are a symbol of Jesus's passion, and the crown
of thorns He had to wear when He was crucified.

David Self

Isaiah, chapter 40, verses 3–5 and 9–11. *The coming or Advent of
Jesus was being prophesied hundreds of years before he was born. In the
eighth century* B.C., *Isaiah was telling his people (in these verses) to
prepare for His coming.*

St Nicholas
(6 December)

———◆◆◆◆———

The custom described in this passage was common in English churches,
abbeys and cathedrals in medieval times.

Each year on the Eve of Saint Nicholas, the patron saint of
children, the choirboys – as a reward perhaps for months of
unpaid work – were permitted by the clergy to choose one of their
number to enact the Boy Bishop. The child elected would be
invested with all the powers of the Bishop himself, and his reign
lasted for a day and a night on the Feast of the Holy Innocents.

It was at vespers, on the eve of the festival, two days after
Christmas, that the Boy Bishop, carrying his pastoral staff and
wearing a miniature cope of gold-embroidered velvet, a jewelled
mitre upon his head, assembled in the church with his small
canons around him. The real canons now led the procession
instead of the choirboys, while the Boy Bishop brought up the
rear.

Solemnly they processed through the candle-lit cathedral,
down the great nave to the altar of the Holy Innocents. Then
slowly they returned to the High Altar, where, as the choir sang
out the words 'He shall put down the mighty from their seat', the
real Bishop descended – and up went the Boy Bishop to sit upon
the throne.

Following the service the Boy Bishop was given a supper by
one of the clergy, and after the feasting he rode by torchlight upon a horse, followed by his canons also on horseback,
to bless the people waiting in the wintry streets to see him
pass by.

The reception given to the Boy Bishop would nowadays only
be afforded to a pop star. The people swarmed around him,
singing and dancing and pulling at his clothes – not only in the

street, but even in the church itself. For to them the Boy Bishop was a mysterious little person; a symbol perhaps of an innocence fast slipping from their grasp.

Katherine Hudson

Festivals of light

Christians associate light most closely with Christmas, when light is a reminder of the Star of Bethlehem and of Jesus himself who said that he was the 'Light of the World' (John chapter 8, verse 12). It was natural for Christians to adapt the Roman Saturnalia to honour the birth of Jesus and because of this many pre-Christian features, remain to this day. The Christian nativity first appeared in Roman calendars in A.D. 336.

Christingle services are becoming increasingly popular in the United Kingdom. They were devised originally by the Moravians who wanted to invent a symbol which was distinctly Christian. A christingle is an orange (symbolizing God's world), surrounded by red ribbon or adhesive tape (symbolizing Christ's blood shed for the world), pierced by four cocktail sticks on which are one or two nuts and raisins (symbolizing the fruits of the world). In the top of the orange is set a small lighted candle with a tin-foil base (symbolizing Jesus, the Light of the World). Children bring gifts to the service and receive in return a lighted christingle as a reminder of the Christian message.

The Hindu festival of Diwali is one in which light is an important symbol. It is usually held in October or November and is a time of thanksgiving to the gods for their provision in the previous year and a time to ask for their blessing in the year that lies ahead. Often houses and temples are filled with lights and lamps and in some places lamps are made to float in harbours, streams and ponds. Children enjoy the festival because of the presents which are exchanged. The legend of Rama and Sita is usually recounted at Diwali. This tells of a young man called Rama and a girl called Sita who are in love with one another. A monster called Ravana seizes Sita and takes her back to the island of Sri Lanka. Rama pursues Ravana and after killing him is reunited with Sita who has constantly been faithful to him. The story depicts the conquest of evil by goodness, or darkness by light, and it gives hope to Hindus that the goodness of God will prevail in the year to come.

Also in December is the Jewish festival of Hannukah, which commemorates the occasion in 164 B.C. when Judas Maccabeus led a resistance movement against King Antiochus in whose reign the Jewish faith was opposed and corrupted. Judas captured the Temple in Jerusalem and cleansed it of foreign influence, so restoring traditional Hebrew worship. In the Temple Judas found one jar of sanctified oil, which he used to light a special lamp there. Miraculously it burnt for eight days, until more oil could be sanctified by the priests. At Hannukah, Jews light a nine-branch candelabrum called a menorah; one candle for each of the eight days and one extra from which the eight can be lit. Jewish boys and girls enjoy the singing, dancing, games and, of course, the lighting of the menorah.

Geoffrey Marshall-Taylor

Christmas

—•◆•—

1: CHRISTMAS IN NAZARETH

Many Christian pilgrims, going to celebrate Christmas in the Holy Land, will chose to spend Christmas Eve in the Galilean town of Nazareth, where Jesus spent his childhood and began his teaching.

Nazareth is a hill town, lying between the Mediterranean and the Sea of Galilee. . . .

It has remained much the same as it was in Biblical times with winding alleyways, steep lanes, and old trees framing time-smoothened stone houses. The atmosphere is one of charm and serenity which is emphasized, indeed even enhanced on Christmas Eve, when church bells peal, carols fill the air and melodic voices are raised in prayer.

But more than all this, there is a special atmosphere created, perhaps by the knowledge of the townspeople – the majority of whom are Christian Arabs – and the pilgrims who go there, that it was at Nazareth that the angel Gabriel appeared to Mary and announced to her the advent of Jesus' birth.

The Basilica of the Annunciation, one of the oldest shrines in the Christian world, stands above the site where the angel appeared to Mary. Beneath the Basilica is the grotto in which two splendidly sculptured granite columns stand on the spots believed to be where Mary and Gabriel faced each other.

Throughout the town are many sites associated with the life of Our Lord – the Church of St Joseph, where Joseph is said to have had his carpentry shop; Mary's Well, where she may have gone to draw water for her family.

As many pilgrims have found, a visit to Nazareth and the Galilee region of Israel, so strongly associated with Jesus' early

166

life and the first years of his ministry, gives the pilgrim a sense of the setting of those events which took place so many years ago but which still shape and affect our life today.

Catholic Herald

Luke, chapter 1, verses 26–38. *It was in Nazareth, where Mary and Joseph lived, that the Angel Gabriel 'announced' the birth of Jesus to Mary.*

2: THE HOMECOMING

At Christmas, many families are reunited. Grown-up children come home to their parents, as does William in a novel by D.H. Lawrence called Sons and Lovers.

Everybody was mad with excitement. William was coming on Christmas Eve. Mrs Morel surveyed the pantry. There was a big plum cake, and a rice cake, jam tarts, lemon tarts, and mince pies – two enormous dishes. Everywhere was decorated. The kissing bunch of berried holly, hung with bright and glittering things, spun slowly over Mrs Morel's head as she trimmed her little tarts in the kitchen. A great fire roared. There was a scent of cooked pastry. He was due at seven o'clock, but he would be late. The three children had gone to meet him. She was alone.

But at a quarter to seven Morel came in again. Neither wife nor husband spoke. He sat in his armchair, quite awkward with excitement, and she quietly went on with her baking. Only by the careful way in which she did things could it be told how much moved she was. The clock ticked on.

'What time dost say he's coming?' Morel asked for the fifth time.

'The train gets in at half past six,' she replied emphatically.

'Then he'll be here at ten past seven.'

'Eh, bless you, it'll be hours late,' she said.

Meantime the three children were on the platform at the railway station, two miles from home. They waited one hour. A train came – he was not there. Down the line the red and green lights shone. It was very dark and very cold.

'Ask him if the London train's come,' said Paul to Annie, when they saw a man in a tip cap.

'I'm not,' said Annie. 'You be quiet – he might send us off.'

But Paul was dying for the man to know they were expecting someone by the London train: it sounded so grand. Yet he was much too much scared of broaching any man, let alone one in a peaked cap, to dare to ask.

They all grew silent. He wasn't coming. They looked down the darkness of the railway. There was London! It seemed the uttermost of distance. They were all too troubled to talk. Cold and unhappy, and silent, they saw the lights of an engine peering round away down the darkness. A porter ran out. The children drew back with beating hearts. A great train bound for Manchester drew up. Two doors opened, and from one of them, William.

D.H. Lawrence

Isaiah, chapter 9, verses 2–6. *For Christians, Advent is a period of waiting for someone special to come, just as the Morel family wait for William.*

When Jesus was born, he brought a message of hope and peace.

Long before he was born, the prophet Isaiah imagined how wonderful it would be when he would be alive.

3: PAGAN CHRISTMAS

The original Christmas party was in honour of Wotan in northern Europe and Saturn in Rome. The hangover lingers on, with many other pagan memories.

Midwinter festivities are far older than Christianity and have appeared in every culture of the northern hemisphere. The early Christians, on controlling Europe, tried to convert pagan ceremonies to Christian purposes but with only partial success. In the resulting tangle, paganism has partially held its own and many objects associated with Christmas are explicable only as deep folk memories.

The root of midwinter rituals is the winter solstice, the shortest day which falls on or around 21 December. In the days before the solstice it was necessary to use propitiatory rituals to prevent the sun getting any weaker. After the solstice, with the day getting longer, was the time for celebration. The actual date of 25 December was that of the Roman festival of the 'unconquered sun' and appears to have been chosen as a deliberate attempt to Christianize that celebration. It is interesting that in Scotland, although the Christmas celebration has advanced in popularity in recent years, the main midwinter festival is still the entirely non-Christian one of Hogmanay, the New Year.

Besides sun worship, today's Christmas festivities reflect a complex of other pagan rites, many distorted from their original purpose. The two chief ones are the Roman Saturnalia and the Germanic-Nordic festivities centering around Wotan and tree worship.

The Roman Saturnalia, held annually on 17 to 19 December, were days of public revelry in honour of the god Saturn. During the Saturnalia all business was suspended and many distinctions of rank were forgotten. Masters sometimes waited on their slaves – a custom reflected to this day in the military custom of officers serving Christmas dinner to their men. Saturn is one of the several ancestors of Father Christmas.

Colin Cross

4: CHRISTMAS CHEER

Now thrice welcome, Christmas,
Which brings us good cheer,
Minced pies and plum porridge,
Good ale and strong beer;
With pig, goose and capon,
The best that can be!

One of the most famous Christmas dinners was the one that the reformed Scrooge provided for the Cratchits, in Charles Dickens' Christmas Carol.

There never was such a goose. Its tenderness and flavour were themes of universal admiration. Eked out by apple sauce and mashed potatoes, it was a sufficient dinner for the whole family: everyone had enough and the youngest Cratchits were steeped in sage and onion to the eyebrows!

But now the plates were being changed and Mrs Cratchit left the room to bring in the pudding.

Suppose it should not be done enough! Suppose somebody should have got over the wall of the backyard and stolen it? But hallo! There's a great deal of steam – a smell like washing day –

that was the cloth. A smell like an eating house and a pastry cook's next door to each other – that was the pudding! In half a minute Mrs Cratchit entered, flushed but smiling proudly, with the pudding like a speckled cannon ball, hard and firm, blazing with brandy and with Christmas holly stuck in the top. It was a wonderful pudding!

Charles Dickens

Turkey is more common than goose nowadays, but the traditional Christmas joint is beef. Two hundred years ago the vicar of Weston Longville near Norwich was celebrating a really traditional Christmas day as he described in his diary.

I read prayers and administered the holy sacrament this morning at Weston, it being Christmas Day. James Smith, my clerk, Richard Buck, Thomas Cushing, Richard Bates, Thomas Dicker and Thomas Carey all dined at my house as usual on Christmas Day. I gave to each of them a shilling to carry home to their wives before they went away and I gave them for dinner a piece of roast beef and plumb puddings and after dinner half a pint of strong beer apiece. N.B. They are all old men.

This evening about nine, I had another tub of gin and another of the best coniac brandy brought me. We heard a thump at the front door about that time, but did not know what it was, till I went out and found the two tubs – but nobody there!

Parson Woodforde

5: SANTA'S CLAUSES

(Santa Claus speaks. . . .)

Dear Sirs,

I am writing to you as my employers in order to make certain points about my conditions of employment which I feel are due for renegotiation.

1 Transport. All the other representatives of my acquaintance are supplied by their firms with a car. I appreciate that a sleigh pulled by reindeer has the charm of tradition but it is hardly the ideal form of locomotion for late December. Also since the P.R. Department's campaign to promote the image of my lead reindeer, he has become very difficult to handle. He considers

himself now to be a superstar, holds an Equity card, and on several occasions recently has incited the other reindeer to militant industrial action, which has led to some perilous arbitration disputes in the sky over Barnsley, Southampton and other densely-populated areas.

2 Uniform.   If you are agreeable to disposing of the means of transport, it will follow that the big red coat and Wellington boots are also superfluous. Given the lack of chimneys and the increased use of small-bore central heating systems, it has become increasingly difficult to gain access to some premises in order to place display material. I feel that a foam-lined, P.V.C. skin-diver's outfit would be much more appropriate. And I would like permission to shave again. Again, I realize the traditional value of the long white beard, but it effectively prohibits my active social life and is, I feel sure, the main reason why I am still a bachelor.

3 Area.   In my conversations with other representatives I have come to realize that my area is much too large. No other firm asks one representative to cover the whole world in one night. I suggest, therefore, that we discontinue the practice of leaving courtesy cards at the homes of Muslims and Buddhists; and that you employ another representative for the Southern Hemisphere. Also, given that the Factories Act requires employees to record a statutory ninety days before they are entitled to take a holiday, I would bring your attention to the fact that at this rate, working one day a year, I shall be 114 before I qualify.

4 Productivity.   The exact figures are not available to me at the moment but I would point out that the world population has increased very considerably of late. And they are all children. Also, with the growth of education and the attendant cynicism, belief in Father Christmas has been eroded. This in itself poses no problem, except that many children, in their desire to obtain evidence to support or refute their theories as to my existence, set big steel traps by the fireplace. I think my salary should reflect this added hazard.

5 Factory.   It has never seemed to me that the North Pole was the ideal site for a factory. I would, therefore, request that the Production Department rethink its strategy. Also, it has never made economic sense in my mind that the factory should be staffed by gnomes. It only needs a child to ask for a tank and forty of them are occupied for a fortnight.

I would therefore, be grateful if you would consider the above points. To sum up: I would suggest that Rudolph be sold to the makers of Lassie; that the factory be re-sited in Monte Carlo and staffed by West Indians, and that Christmas be staggered.

Yours faithfully,
S. Claus

C.A. McLaren and W.J.S. Kirton

Epiphany
(6 January)

The Christian Feast of the Epiphany marks the coming of the Wise Men to the infant Jesus. They were, according to the Gospel, the first non-Jews to worship Jesus. How true is the story?

The star? This is an emblem which appears over and over again in Jewish thought of the period. It dated back to the prophecy of Balaam in the Book of Numbers: 'A star shall come forth out of Jacob'. In the Dead Sea Scrolls, one of the expected Messiahs is called 'the star' and he is to be the interpreter of the Law.

The Wise Men? The Greek word in Matthew really signifies 'astrologers'. 'From the East' means, presumably, from Mesopotamia or Persia, the homes of the Zoroastrian faith, a religion which, with its angels, its conflict between darkness and light and its teaching on the immortality of the human soul, appears profoundly to have influenced Judaism. Heaven and hell were, originally, Zoroastrian ideas.

Although, in mainstream Christian tradition, the wise men are referred to as 'kings', there is no scriptural warranty for their being that.

In the early Church the Feast of the Epiphany, commemorating the wise men and Jesus's baptism, was more important than Jesus's birthday. It was not until about A.D. 330 that Christmas was recognized as a feast. The importance of it grew as part of a conscious policy of Christianizing the pagan midwinter rites which had already long existed. The first model crib, for placing in church, appears to have been made by St Francis of Assisi as late as 1224.

So by a rich combination of tradition, legend and interpretation there developed the Christian Christmas.

Colin Cross

173

Plough Monday

———◆•◆———

Plough Monday, the first Monday after Twelfth Day, was celebrated in most East Anglian villages by men and boys, with blackened faces, dragging a plough through their respective villages and threatening to plough up the doorstep or garden path of anyone so ungenerous as to refuse them money. Until 1929, in the Cambridgeshire village of Swaffham Prior, schoolboys blackened their faces and took round a miniature plough. A resident recalled how 'we visited the more well-to-do homes and sang at each one:

> A sifting of chaff, a bottle of hay,
> See the poor colts go carrying away.
> Squeak, boys, squeak, and wag your tails,
> Hi ninney, Hi nonney.

The 'Hi' was shouted as loud as we could yell. One farmer would make us come up, one by one, and present us with a sixpence which, once grasped firmly in the hand, we would turn and run as hard as we could with the farmer's hearty laughter and his huge whip cracking at our heels.'

In the same county, as Wimpole, the men with the plough carried whips which they cracked enthusiastically as they toured the village. At each door they gathered in a group and, with much whip-cracking, shouted:

> Up with your scrapers and down with your doors,
> If you don't give us money we won't plough no more.

In Whittlesford the day was known as Tiddle-lol-day from the custom, continued to the 1870s, of black-faced boys going round the village asking for money and chanting 'tiddle lol, tiddle lol, tiddle lol, lol, tol'; the ploughmen collected their money in the

174

evening. In Doddington and other villages in north-east Cambridgeshire the day was known as Plough Witching Day, a name not yet forgotten, and the taking round of the plough as 'going plough-witching'.

Morris or Molly dancing was an important part of the day's festivities, performed in the evening in many villages, by men with coloured rosettes on their jackets. The Molly or Bessie, clad in a woman's long dress and befeathered hat, ususally collected the money, often in a wooden ladle.

At one time men from the villages nearest to Cambridge, wearing green sashes round their shoulders and waists, and accompanied by fiddlers, used to dance into Cambridge on Plough Monday morning to dance in the market place. By the final years of the last century, however, this 'invasion' of Cambridge took place in the later afternoon and early evening and had degenerated into a somewhat rough affair with no dancing. Many elderly residents can recall being frightened, as children, by the gangs of noisy, black-faced and often intoxicated men and youths who paraded the streets demanding money, which was at once spent in the nearest public house.

Plough Monday was the day on which East Anglian ploughboys were initiated as members of the plough team. The ceremony was usually performed by the ploughmen tapping on the soles of the initiates' shoes, but in the Norfolk Fens the boy was first chased by the men who then grabbed him and pressed his face against the tail of a horse. Much beer drinking, of course, accompanied both forms of the ceremony.

Enid Porter

St Paul
(25 January)

———◆◆◆◆———

In the Christian calendar, 25 January is the Feast of the Conversion of St Paul. He was born in Tarsus in what is now southern Turkey. He was a Greek Jew who was converted to Christianity in a moment of vision on the road between Jerusalem and Damascus, in A.D. 37. In that moment he changed from persecutor of the Christians into their most energetic and effective spokesman. He wrote half the New Testament and his ideas lie at the roots of Western culture. His missionary journeys took him across the then-known world.

Paul was born about A.D. 10 which made him about fourteen years younger than Jesus of Nazareth, whom he never met. Jesus's background appears to have been rural and proletarian. Paul belonged to a well-to-do family in a sophisticated urban setting; the family had the status of Roman citizens, which would have put them among the upper crust. Paul presumably would have had a sound general education in Greek culture, although his letters show no evidence of a love of the classics, and would have had his early religious training in the local Greek-speaking Jewish synagogue.

Paul, it can be assumed, was an exceptionally religious boy. In his mid-teens he left home to embark on a prolonged course of religious study at Jerusalem, the centre of his faith. This was an ordinary way of becoming qualified as a rabbi, that is as a scholar-teacher who depended upon his learning rather than upon any mystical priestly status.

Paul came into contact with the 'Disciples of Jesus' in about A.D. 36, that is roughly six years after the customarily accepted date of the crucifixion.

Then in his mid-twenties, Paul must have advanced far in his religious studies and probably his energy and ability had marked him out as a promising man. His initial attitude to the Jesus group was one of revulsion and, by his own account, he played a leading part in persecuting it (including the death of Stephen).

Shortly after the lynching of Stephen, Paul set off for Damascus with some kind of commission to persecute a Jewish Messianic group there which was either a branch of the 'Disciples of Jesus' or closely akin to them. This was in the winter of A.D. 36–7. Somewhere on the road – the exact spot is unknown – he experienced a vision of Jesus which set him on his main life's work.

There are three accounts of the vision, differing in detail, but all agree on the main points. At midday, Paul felt himself surrounded by a bright light that blinded him. A voice said: 'Saul, Saul, why are you persecuting me?' He answered: 'Who are you, Lord?' The voice said: 'I am Jesus the Nazarene and you are persecuting me.'

From that moment Paul was convinced that Jesus was the Christ and he spent the rest of his life preaching this.

Colin Cross

Acts, chapter 9, verses 1–19 *describe the conversion of Paul.*

Lent

Until recently, all adult Catholics in good health were required to abstain from eating meat on Fridays as a penance and as a reminder that this was the day of Christ's death. There now only remain, in England at least, two days of abstinence – Ash Wednesday, the first day of Lent, and Good Friday. These two days are also the only two remaining days of fasting. Fasting does not mean, as it does in some other religions, that Catholics must refrain from eating altogether, but their meals are limited by certain stringent regulations the details of which every Catholic must know. At one time there were very many fast days, particularly during Lent. Now, for a number of reasons, perhaps not least being the need to keep physically abreast of the pace of modern life, these have been abolished.

Peter Kelly

Ash Wednesday begins Lent. It was so named because of the ancient custom of sprinkling ashes on the forehead of Churchmen mindful of their sins. *Shrove Tuesday*, before it, is traditionally the day on which sinners are 'shriven' or absolved.

Lent is the period of forty weekdays before Easter. (It is called 'Lent' from the Anglo-Saxon word for Spring). It is associated with the forty days spent by Jesus in the desert after his baptism, thinking out the question of what should be the nature of his work. He was surrounded by devilish temptations to choose the easy ways of sensationalism and power, instead of the way which he did take – the way of humility and service, the way which led to the cross.

It is the ancient custom of Churchmen to give up some pleasures during Lent. It is a token of their wish to be with our Lord in the hardness which he chose. Above all, Churchmen try in Lent to set aside more time for prayer and for the study of Christianity, particularly of the Bible.

The fourth Sunday in Lent has a cheerful note, being called 'Refreshment Sunday'. This is also called *Mothering Sunday*, when we thank God for our own mothers and families, and for the Church as the mother of Christians.

The fifth Sunday is *Passion Sunday*, when we think of the suffering ('passion' originally meant suffering) through which Jesus founded the Church.

Next comes *Palm Sunday*, when we recall the triumphant entry of Jesus into Jerusalem, with the crowd waving the branches of palm trees. Palm leaves made into crosses are distributed in many churches on this day.

From Palm Sunday to Easter is *Holy Week*. This includes *Maundy Thursday*, the day of the Last Supper. *Mandatum*, the origin of 'Maundy', is the Latin for 'commandment' –the 'new commandment' of love, expressed by Jesus through his washing the feet of the disciples and through his founding of Holy Communion. And the climax of the week is *Good Friday*, the day of the Crucifixion.

David L. Edwards

Matthew, chapter 4, verses 1–11 *(and also* Luke, chapter 4, verses 1–13) *describe the temptation of Jesus.*

Mothering Sunday

MOTHER AND SON

This is part of a story set in Ireland. It is a reminder of the love that a mother has for her child, a love that may sometimes show itself in apparently strange ways.

Brigid Gill was alone in her cottage waiting for her son to come home from school. He was now an hour late, and as he was only nine she was very nervous about him especially as he was her only child and he was a wild boy always getting into mischief, mitching (or playing truant) from school, fishing minnows on Sunday and building stone 'castles' in the great crags above the village. She kept telling herself that she would give him a good scolding and beating when he came in, but at the same time her heart was thumping with anxiety and she started at every sound, rushing out the door and looking down the winding road, that was now dim with the shadows of the evening. So many things could happen to him.

His dinner of dried fish and roast potatoes was being kept warm in the oven among the peat ashes beside the fire on the hearth, and on the table there was a plate, a knife and a little mug full of buttermilk.

At last she heard the glad cries of the schoolboys afar off, and rushing out she saw them scampering, not up the road, but across the crags to the left, their caps in their hands.

'Thank God,' she said, and then she persuaded herself that she was very angry. Hurriedly she got a small dried willow rod, sat down on a chair within the door and waited for Stephen.

He advanced up the yard very slowly, walking near the stone fence that bounded the vegetable garden, holding his satchel in his left hand by his side. He knew his mother would be angry.

180

At last he reached the door and, holding down his head, he entered the kitchen. The mother immediately jumped up and seized him by the shoulder. The boy screamed, dropped his satchel and his cap and clung to her apron. The mother raised the rod to strike, but when she looked down at the trembling body, she began to tremble herself and dropped the stick. Stooping down, she raised him up and began kissing him, crying at the same time with tears in her eyes.

'What's going to become of you at all, at all? God save us, I haven't the courage to beat you and you're breaking my heart with your wickedness.'

Liam O'Flaherty

The Passover

Passover, the great Jewish Festival of Freedom, has many striking and illustrative symbols which bring home to all who celebrate it from the young to the oldest the great moral and ethical lessons which permeate its continuing history year by year. As the family sit around the table with guests present at the famous Seder (Hebrew: Order) home service, all present can with imagination recapture the four centuries of slavery which were endured by their ancestors.

The youngest person present asks the time honoured question: 'Why is this night different from all other nights?' and the father or the celebrant of this magnificent occasion replies: (because) 'We were slaves under Pharaoh in Egypt and God brought us forth (our ancestors) out of Egypt.'

On the table are the symbolical reminders of the events which reduced a free people to the level of a down-trodden humanity who cried to God to relieve them and who, but for Moses, would have lost their faith completely. They were almost ground into the dust of ancient Egypt. The bitter herbs on the table are used as an expression of the intense suffering of slavery throughout history. The unleavened bread called Matzah, eaten throughout the Passover festival, is a reminder of the affliction of slavery and also of hope of better things since it was prepared hurriedly on the way from the land of slavery towards the wilderness, when Pharaoh was compelled to let God's people go; then in their march to freedom the unleavened bread could very suitably be called the 'Bread of Song'. The redemption of the ancient people of Israel by their heavenly Father is recalled by the shankbone which is a recollection of the Paschal lamb eaten on the very night of delivery.

With so much hunger and poverty in the so called affluent

world of today it is very suitable that at the Seder table there is extended the invitation, 'Let all who are hungry come and eat'. Indeed this is surely a lesson for our times with recent grim applications. Unless people are free from want how can they ever achieve the freedom which is so much emphasized throughout Judaism!

Myer Domnitz

Exodus, chapter 12 *describes the first Passover.*

The Crucifixion

1: ASLAN

In a story called The Lion, the Witch and the Wardrobe *by C.S. Lewis, the lion (who is called Aslan) is put to death by a witch and her attendant hags. In many ways, the death of Aslan is similar to the crucifixion of Jesus.*

'Bind him, I say!' repeated the White Witch. The Hags made a dart at him and shrieked with triumph when they found that he made no resistance at all. Then others – evil dwarfs and apes – rushed in to help them, and between them they rolled the huge lion over on his back and tied all his four paws together, shouting and cheering as if they had done something brave, though, had the Lion chosen, one of those paws could have been the death of them all. But he made no noise, even when the enemies, straining and tugging, pulled the cords so tight that they cut into his flesh. Then they began to drag him towards the Stone Table. . . .

And they surged round Aslan, jeering at him, saying things like 'Puss, Puss! Poor Pussy,' and 'How many mice have you caught today, Cat?' and 'Would you like a saucer of milk, Pussums?'

'Muzzle him!' said the Witch. And even now, as they worked about his face putting on the muzzle, one bite from his jaws would have cost two or three of them their hands. But he never moved. And this seemed to enrage all that rabble. Everyone was at him now: he was surrounded by the whole crowd of creatures kicking him, hitting him, spitting on him, jeering at him.

When once Aslan had been tied (and tied so that he was really a mass of cords) on the flat stone, a hush fell on the crowd. Four Hags, holding four torches, stood at the corners of the Table. The Witch began to whet her knife. It looked, when the gleam of the torchlight fell on it, as if the knife were made of stone, not of steel, and it was of a strange and evil shape.

At last she drew near. She stood by Aslan's head. Her face was working and twitching with passion, but his looked up at the sky, still quiet, neither angry nor afraid, but a little sad. Then, just before she gave the blow, she stooped down and said in a quivering voice,

'And now, who has won? Fool, did you think that by all this you would save the human traitor?'

C.S. Lewis

Jesus has just been tried by the Roman governor, Pontius Pilate, and in this passage the soldiers take Jesus to be crucified. (See also page 190 and Matthew, chapter 27, verses 27–42.)

2: JESUS OF NAZARETH

In Jesus of Nazareth, *Professor William Barclay retells the story of Jesus. In this passage we hear how Jesus was taken to the hill outside Jerusalem, called Calvary. (In a Roman crucifixion, the prisoner was made to carry the crossbeam of his own cross to the place of execution.)*

Jesus, with the crown of thorns still pressing into his head, was taken to the fortress woodyard to be saddled with this crushing burden. . . .

The guards, weary of the hostility of the crowd, began systematically prodding Jesus to make him move faster. At last, weak to the point of utter exhaustion, he stumbled and fell. Struggling up he shakily tried to regain his balance, but fell again. A woman emerged from the crowd and mercifully wiped the sweat and blood from his face. His sight cleared for a moment, and he gazed at her face as if to memorize its features. Then he stumbled forward once more.

At last they reached Calvary.

There was a disturbance in the crowd. John and Martha, their faces drawn and pale from sleepless anguish, pushed forward to get as near to him as possible. Jesus lay on the ground, and his hands were nailed to the cross piece to which he was also bound. With professional expertise the soldiers had soon completed their work. Then he was hoisted up and his feet were fastened to the upright. Nicodemus, who had followed with the crowd, was still murmuring to himself. 'God so loved the world that he sent his only begotten son. . . .'

Pilate's sign had gone up over the cross, 'Jesus of Nazareth, King of the Jews'. Some Pharisees pressed forward, protesting bitterly. 'It's an insult. Blasphemy. Pull down that inscription. He's not the King of the Jews.' The Roman soldiers ignored them and then, when they grew more importunate, thrust them back into the crowd.

Mary, the mother of Jesus, Martha and Mary of Magdala were trying to make their way through the crowd to the foot of the cross, but those in front were intent on mocking Jesus, and kept pushing them back.

A voice cried, 'If you are what you say you are, why don't you come down from the cross?' Another called, 'He saved others, but can't save himself.' Yet another, 'Show us a miracle. We're all waiting.'

William Barclay

Luke, chapter 23, verses 33–46. *This passage from Luke's gospel continues the account of the crucifixion.*

3: ROMAN CRUCIFIXION

These two short passages describe a Roman crucifixion.

(a)   When a man was condemned to this death, first of all he was scourged – tied to an X-like wooden frame in such a way that his back was bent so that he could not move, then thirty-nine lashes were laid on. The lash was a long leather thong, studded at intervals with sharpened bits of bone and pellets of lead, and it literally tore a man's back to shreds: few retained their consciousness, many went mad and not a few died. After that the person had to take upon his back the heavy crosspiece of his cross; Jesus staggered and fell under it. Put in the centre of a square of four Roman soldiers, he was taken in that way to the place of crucifixion by every possible street, square and avenue – the longest possible way – in order that people might see and be terrified at what happens to crime.

(b) The victim was tied with ropes or nailed through the wrists to the wooden crosspiece. The most secure method of fixing him was by twisting his arms behind this spar. Finally, the spar was attached to an upright post already planted in the ground. The shape was either the familiar + or T, the latter being more convenient and so more likely to have been used. There was no need to nail the feet but a peg was knocked in to give support between the legs.

The position was agonizing, every breath requiring intense effort. Even so, some victims took as long as three days to die. Jesus, according to the Gospels lasted the unusually short period of three hours. Was he a man of weak physique? Or had the beating been too severe? These questions are unanswerable, but, for certain, to hang up a man in public and leave him to die was the most contemptuous form of execution it is possible to devise.

The Observer

John, chapter 19, verses 17–24. *This is how John describes the crucifixion of Jesus.*

4: LET'S GO TO GOLGOTHA

This reading is part of a story called Let's go to Golgotha *by Garry Kilworth. Set in the future, it is about two couples who go on a package tour, back in time, to the day of the crucifixion. Simon and his wife have joined in the shouting for the death of Jesus; now they try to join their friends, Harry and Sarah, who have been present at the crucifixion itself.*

In the distance they could hear the crowd chanting and jeering; they could hear the shrieks of laughter and high-pitched catcalls. It was an ugly, frightening sound, like the screaming of monkeys as a lion pads beneath their trees. It was the forced laughter of hyenas that circle the lion's den at a safe distance as the lord lies, unconcerned, in the warm sun. Then, suddenly, there was silence.

Simon slowed, gasping for breath. He could see the rut made by the corner of the cross snaking along the street and disappearing into the distance. A shudder went through him.

'My God,' he sobbed to his wife, 'we've killed him.'

A sandal slipped from his foot as he ran but he disregarded it. He felt none of the sharp stones that cut the soles and heels of his feet.

The pair of them stumbled on, following the tell-tale mark in the dust, until they reached the crowd. The faces were all turned in one direction and wore expressions of shocked sympathy. Simon did not dare look towards the crosses. He knew he would faint if he did, and he had seen the shadows out of the corner of his eye.

It was enough. They found Harry and Sarah on the edge of the crowd, as silent and watchful as the others. Sarah's cheeks were blotched with white and Harry's mouth was half-open.

'Harry,' choked Simon, as quickly as his emotion would allow, 'Harry, we've got to get him down.'

Harry's stunned mind took time to register the fact that Simon was with them once more. He did not take his eyes from the man on the centre cross.

Licking his lips, he replied helplessly, 'Can't do it, Simon. It's got to happen, you know. This is the way it is, but my God, I wish we had never come. He looked at me, you know. I'll never forget his eyes as long as I live.'

Garry Kilworth

Luke, chapter 23, verses 47–9. *These three verses describe the reactions of some of the spectators at the crucifixion.*

5: THE BURIAL

After Jesus died on the cross, his body was buried in a tomb belonging to a rich man from Arimathaea called Joseph. The chief priest of the Jews, Caiaphas, was still worried about Jesus and his followers, and so he visited the Roman governor (or 'procurator') Pilate, in order to ask a favour.

'I have a further request, Your Excellency, which concerns this false prophet, Jesus. He said – you may have heard – that he would rise from the dead.'

'Rise from the dead!' ejaculated Pilate. 'Not after he's had a Roman spear through his heart. Why do you trouble me about such impossible nonsense?'

'I agree, my dear Procurator, that Jesus's claim to rise from the dead is impossible nonsense, as you say. Unfortunately, it is the kind of impossible nonsense he dealt in; the stock in trade with which he deceived multitudes. His followers were always telling tales of the marvels and miracles he performed. And it is not at all impossible that they could steal his dead body, hide it away, and give out that he had risen from the dead and was continuing his mission in secret. Issuing orders for the foolish rabble through them.'

'You think that a serious possibility?' said Pilate. 'Well, what is it that you want me to do?'

'Let the man's burial place be guarded for a short time. From what I hear he said he would rise from the dead in three days. Three seems to have been his magical number. He said he would destroy the Temple and rebuild it in three days. A few days' watch – that's all that will be needed. His followers won't dare to approach with Roman soldiers standing by. Then the story will be discredited and his followers finished. The whole sorry business will be at an end.'

Pilate reflected again, and then shrugged. 'It all seems very far-fetched,' he said, 'but I know how rumours grow.'

He was about to add 'especially in this fanatical priest-ridden hole' but stopped himself in time. 'Very well,' he said, 'if you insist on guards, guards it shall be. I will give the order.'

William Barclay

Matthew, chapter 28, verses 57–66. *These verses are Matthew's account of the above events.*

Easter

1: ASLAN

In the story The Lion, the Witch and the Wardrobe *by C. S. Lewis (see page 184, the lion, Aslan, is put to death on a stone table by a witch. Next morning, two girls, Susan and Lucy (who have been his friends) visit the Table.*

The rising of the sun had made everything look so different – all the colours and shadows were changed – that for a moment they didn't see the important thing. Then they did. The Stone Table was broken into two pieces by a great crack that ran down it from end to end; and there was no Aslan.

'Oh, oh, oh!' cried the two girls, rushing back to the Table. 'Oh, it's too bad', sobbed Lucy; 'they might have left the body alone.'

'Who's done it?' cried Susan. 'What does it mean? Is it more magic?'

'Yes!' said a great voice behind their backs. 'It is more magic.'

They looked round. There, shining in the sunrise, larger than they had seen him before, shaking his mane (for it had apparently grown again) stood Aslan himself.

'Oh, Aslan!' cried the children, staring up at him, almost as much frightened as they were glad.

'Aren't you dead then, dear Aslan?' said Lucy.

'Not now,' said Aslan.

'You're not – not a – ?' asked Susan in a shaky voice. She couldn't bring herself to say the word ghost. Aslan stooped his golden head and licked her forehead. The warmth of his breath and a rich sort of smell that seemed to hang about his hair came all over her.

'Do I look it?' he said.

'Oh, you're real, you're real! Oh, Aslan!' cried Lucy, and both girls flung themselves upon him and covered him with kisses.

'But what does it all mean?' asked Susan when they were somewhat calmer.

'It means,' said Aslan, 'that though the Witch knew the Deep Magic, there is a magic deeper still which she did not know. Her knowledge goes back only to the dawn of time. But if she could have looked a little further back, into the stillness and the darkness before time dawned, she would have read there a different incantation. She would have known that when a willing victim who had committed no treachery was killed in a traitor's stead, the Table would crack and Death itself would start working backwards. And now –'

'Oh yes. Now?' said Lucy, jumping up and clapping her hands.

'Oh, children,' said the Lion, 'I feel my strength coming back to me. Oh, children, catch me if you can!'

C.S. Lewis

Matthew, chapter 28, verses 1–8. *These verses tell how two of Jesus's followers visited his tomb and discovered that he had risen from the dead (like Aslan in the story above).*

2: THE DAVIDSON AFFAIR

In a modern story, The Davidson Affair, *the author, Stuart Jackman, updates the Bible story. Jesus, son of David becomes Jesus Davidson, the one-time prostitute Mary Magdalene becomes Miss Magdala, a modern call-girl.*

In this episode, a television interviewer recalls his attempt to interview Miss Magdala, after she found the tomb empty on the first Easter morning.

Mary Magdala sat in the chair with an easy grace, her hands folded composedly in her lap. . . .

'Miss Magdala,' I said then, 'thank you first of all for coming.'

She nodded. 'I'm glad to be here.'

'It's very good of you.'

'The fact is,' I said carefully, 'we're trying to establish the truth about Jesus Davidson.'

'Yes,' she said, her voice low and clear.

'I wonder if you could tell us what happened then, Miss Magdala? At the tomb, I mean.'

'He broke out. Nothing they could do could hold him.' She laughed, spreading her hands in a gesture of excitement. 'They sealed up the tomb, you know, and mounted a guard. It was ridiculous. Pathetic. Like tying-up a sleeping lion with cotton thread. When he wakened he just snapped the thread and strode out.'

'You say you saw him there, outside the tomb?'

'I did indeed.'

'Alive?'

'Of course.'

'Miss Magdala,' I said brutally, 'I'm sorry, but that's just not possible.'

She was quite unshaken. 'It's a miracle. Mr Tennel. They come naturally to him, of course. I'm ashamed to think how slow we've been to recognize this.'

'It's understandable,' I said. 'I'm not much for miracles myself.'

'He performed many, Mr Tennel. A great many.'

'So I'm told.'

'The trouble is, people misunderstood them.'

'Didn't believe in them, you mean?'

'Oh, no. They believed all right. If you see a cripple get up and walk, and listen to a deaf-mute you've known all your life suddenly start singing, you haven't much option, have you? When it happens like that, in front of a crowd, you've got to believe it. . . . It was the meaning of what he did they couldn't understand. They thought he was just a man doing something extraordinary.'

'Yes,' I said.

'No. That's exactly the point. He wasn't an ordinary man. He was God. God in person, doing the things that came naturally to him. People always said,"How can this 'village nobody' work miracles?" But the real question is "How can God walk about Israel like a man?" That's the basic miracle, Mr Tennel, that he was here at all. Once you've seen that, the rest is perfectly logical.'

'Even a resurrection?'

'Especially that. Death can't hold God.'

Stuart Jackman

Mark, chapter 16, verses 1–11. *Mark's account of the resurrection tells how Mary Magdalene visited the tomb on the first Easter morning.*

Easter in the
Orthodox Church

⬥·◆·◆·⬥

*The Eastern Church fixes the date of Easter by a different method to that
of the Western Church, and the two do not always coincide.*

Easter, the feast of feasts, is reached by way of Holy Week.
During this week, the church services bring the Orthodox Christians step by step from the entry into Jerusalem, through the Last
Supper and the Garden of Gethsemane, to the Crucifixion and
the burial of Christ.

Most of the services are centred on readings from the Gospels.
Perhaps the most impressive and most moving moments are
those when these readings are acted out.

On Thursday that week, the day of the Last Supper, the original Last Supper is marked by people sharing in its continuation,
the Communion. And if a bishop is present, he will also mark the
Last Supper by publicly washing the feet of his assistant priests,
just as Christ washed the feet of his disciples. The following
evening, night or early morning are set aside for the reading of
the Gospels which tell of Christ's sufferings during those hours.
And when the sufferings are over, Christ's descent from the
Cross is acted out.

On the afternoon of Good Friday, a slow procession makes its
way from the altar to the centre of the church. The priest or
bishop solemnly carries a cloth on which is painted or embroid-
ered an icon (or picture) of the dead Christ. He lowers it onto a
stand in the middle of the building. As at an ordinary funeral,
people stand with lighted candles. They bow before the icon and
they kiss it.

Later, the icon is taken in procession round the outside of the
church, with the worshippers following as mourners, while the
bells are tolled. The cloth is brought back to the centre of the
church to mark the burial itself.

But the burial is not the end of the story. Already at this service late Friday evening or early Saturday morning, some of the readings and chants hint at the resurrection to come. These hints grow more insistent at the Eucharist on Saturday morning. Up until now the clergy have been wearing solemn, black vestments. Just before the Gospel reading these are suddenly exchanged for festive white ones. And the Gospel itself speaks already of the women at the tomb of Christ who find it empty, and their Saviour risen.

At midnight, in the first moments of Easter Day, the story is taken up again. Just as the women came to the tomb, so clergy and people come in procession to the church. They circle the building and pause before the main doors of the building, which are closed.

The mystery of Christ's tomb is about to be revealed. But for the moment the closed doors represent the great stone which the women at the tomb expected to bar their entrance.

Inside the church the icon of the buried Christ has already been removed to the altar.

Outside, the candles flickering in the cool night air, the people wait for the minister to give the blessing. And then they hear, three times repeated, the triumphant announcement of Christ's victory over death. 'Christ is risen from the dead: By death he has trampled down death: And to those who are in the grave he has given life.'

The people repeat the chant. Bells are pealed. In some countries (Greece, for instance) sirens join in, guns are fired and fireworks are exploded.

The doors swing open. The procession sweeps in. It is a moment of enormous joy. And the source of that joy is indicated over and over again. Throughout the next part of the service, and throughout the Easter season, Orothodox Christians greet each other cheerfully with the words, 'Christ is risen', and with the answer to this greeting – 'Risen indeed!'

Sergei Hackel

This is another description of Easter in a Greek Orthodox church.

Towards midnight on Saturday the whole community (except for widows and those in mourning) assembles in and around the church – all bringing unlighted candles. The schoolboys carry

Roman candles and fire-crackers besides. Only the earliest comers can see and hear the service in progress, until the priest, holding a lighted candle, interrupts it to come out of doors and mount a platform under the stars. He is chanting the Gospel story of the Resurrection. It is almost midnight. Now he sings, 'Come ye, partake of the never-setting Light!' The clear flames dance and spread out, passing from candle to candle – like the sparkling of a dark sea under an invisible rising sun – until every candle in the crowd is alight. Finally midnight comes, and the priest cries out, 'Christos Anesti!' ('Christ is Risen!') The sea of candle flames lifts up.

Suddenly every church bell and ship's siren in the whole of Greece sounds forth. Now the candles dip and weave amid the first crackling blossoms of fireworks as the people embrace each other repeating and repeating 'Christos Anesti!'

Alexander Eliot

Luke, chapter 24, verses 1–12 *give another account of the Resurrection.*

May Day

—·◆·◆·◆·—

1: IN CORNWALL

The First of May is inaugurated with much uproar. As soon as the clock has told of midnight, a loud blast on tin trumpets proclaims the advent of May. This is long continued. At day-break, with their 'tintarrems', they proceed to the country, and strip the sycamore trees (called May-trees) of all their young branches, to make whistles. With these shrill musical instruments they return home. Young men and women devote May Day to junketing and picnics.

It was a custom at Penzance, and probably at many other Cornish towns, when the author was a boy, for a number of young people to sit up until twelve o'clock, and then to march round the town with violins, and fifes, and summon their friends to the Maying.

When all were gathered, they went into the country, and were welcomed at the farmhouses at which they called, with some refreshment in the shape of rum and milk, junket, or something of that sort.

Then they gathered the 'May', which included the young branches of any tree in blossom or fresh leaf. The branches of the sycamore were especially cut for the purpose of making 'May-music'. This was done by cutting a circle through the bark to the wood a few inches from the end of the branch. The bark was wetted and carefully beaten until it was loosened and could be slid off from the wood. The wood was cut angularly at the end, so as to form a mouthpiece, and a slit was made in both the bark and the wood, so that when the bark was replaced a whistle was formed.

Prepared with a sufficient number of May whistles, all the

party returned to the town, the band playing, whistles blowing and the young people singing some appropriate song.

Robert Hunt

2: A PURITAN VIEW

May Day has had its critics. This passage was written in 1583.

Against May, Whitsunday, or some other time of the year, every parish, town and village assemble themselves together, both men, women and children, old and young, even all indifferently; and either going all together or dividing themselves into companies, they go some to the woods and groves, some to the hills and mountains, some to one place and some to another, where they spend all the night in pleasant pastimes; and in the morning they return, bringing with them birch boughs and branches of trees, to deck their assemblies withal. And no marvel, for there is a great lord amongst them, as superintendent and lord over their pastimes and sports, namely Satan, prince of hell. But their chiefest jewel they bring from thence is their Maypole, which they bring home with great veneration, as thus. They have twenty or forty yoke of oxen, every ox having a sweet nosegay of flowers placed on the tip of his horns: and these oxen draw home this maypole (this stinking idol, rather) which is covered all over with flowers and herbs, bound round about with strings from the top to the bottom, and sometime painted with variable colours, with two or three hundred men, women and children following it with great devotion.

And thus being reared up with handkerchiefs and flags streaming on the top, they straw the ground about, bind green boughs about it, set up summer-halls, bowers, and arbours hard by it, and then they fall to banquet and feast, to leap and dance about it; as the heathen people did at the dedication of their idols, whereof this is a perfect pattern, or rather the thing itself.

Philip Stubbes

Christian Aid
Week

———◆◆◆———

Christian Aid is a division of the British Council of Churches which aims to provide aid for the poorer nations of the world, for refugees and victims of disasters. Christian Aid Week is held annually in May.

1: A QUESTION OF PRIORITIES

Enter five readers with newspaper headlines on banners or posters.

Reader 1: EARTHQUAKE KILLS 20,000 IN IRAN.

Reader 2: OVER A THOUSAND DROWN IN WORST INDIAN FLOODS THIS CENTURY.

Reader 3: MILLIONS OF PEOPLE WITH HOOKWORM . . . W.H.O. REPORT SEEKS NEW CAMPAIGN.

Reader 4: A THIRD OF THE WORLD INADEQUATELY FED . . . F.A.O. REPORT DEMANDS ACTION.

Reader 5: REFUGEES BOMBED AND MANY KILLED IN TERROR RAID ON CAMP.

Leader: What's your reaction to these newspaper headlines?

Reader 1: Gawd, another assembly about the starving millions – not again for heaven's sake.

Reader 2: Well, they should take more flood prevention measures. But they're used to it anyhow, so it doesn't really matter.

Reader 3: One way of sorting out the population problem.

Reader 4: We can't actually send them our food, so they had better grow more of their own.

Reader 5: There's nothing we can do about it – it's miles away, they'd better look after themselves.

Leader: Not every teenager can run away from the problems of the world.

Reader 3: Towards the end of the Second World War, as the Nazi regime faced increasing pressure from armies of the Allies,

198

German teenagers were forced into the Nazi army – the S.S. Refusal meant execution: this was a decision of life and death for many.

Here is the last letter of a teenager who worked on a farm in Germany in February 1944:

Reader 2: 3 February 1944

Dear Parents: I must give you bad news – I have been condemned to death, I and Gustave G. We did not sign up for the S.S., and so they condemned us to death. You wrote me, indeed, that I should not join the S.S.; my comrade, Gustave G., did not sign up either. Both of us would rather die than stain our consciences with such deeds of horror. I know what the S.S. has to do. Oh, my dear parents, difficult as it is for me and for you, forgive me and pray for me. If I were to be killed in the war while my conscience was bad, that too would be sad for you.

Many more parents will lose their children. Many S.S. men will get killed too. I thank you for everything you have done for my good since my childhood; forgive me, pray for me. . . .

Reader 4: We are spared this kind of decision but there are plenty of teenagers who have recently taken decisions which decide their future.

Reader 5: In Botswana there are many teenagers, of both sexes, who have fled from the injustice of South Africa. They have left family and friends and live on a meagre allowance from the Botswana Refugee Council to which Christian Aid contributes. These students need textbooks, clothing, cash for food, paper and pencils.

Reader 1: Similarly, there are many young refugees from Rhodesia/Zimbabwe living in camps in Mozambique and Zambia in desperate need of equipment. In 1978 Christian Aid sent 10,000 exercise books, 4000 pencils, 1000 rulers and four typewriters for one group of refugees in Southern Africa.

Reader 5: A prayer.

Let us think quietly about those who have to take big decisions so early in their lives.

Reader 4: Let us remember those teenagers whose lives have been ruined by warfare and strife. . .

In Cambodia . . . in Vietnam . . .

In Zimbabwe . . . in Angola . . . in Argentina . . .

Reader 3: Let us realize our responsibilities

Let us have the imagination to understand. . .
    the will to persevere . . .
    and the courage to act in the ways we can,
    particularly during this Christian Aid Week.

Christian Aid

2: CHILD POWER

*As the assembly opens as many children as is practicable should appear
from different directions, each carrying a bucket of water, and converge at
a central point . . . then the assembly will begin.*

Reader 1: As dawn breaks in countries in Asia and Africa, a huge
international gang is on the move. Hundreds of thousands,
assembled in little platoons, march off to work.

Reader 2: This is the gang of water carriers who twice a day
queue around taps and pumps to fetch water vital for the
home.

Reader 3: This is a children's workforce. They struggle with the
weight of water. Every gallon weighs ten pounds – buckets and
tubs pull at straining limbs – their tummies are often empty,
but the water must be got home.

Reader 4: There's not a pipe in the house – nor that house, nor
that house nor that house – the nearest pipe is a quarter of a
mile away and sometimes that's switched off.

Reader 5: If only . . . if only we had a tap with clean water – that's
not asking for much.

Reader 1: We take taps for granted in the UK; there's a whole
elaborate system to provide us with clean safe water. London's
Thames drinking water has already been used several times
upstream before Londoners swallow it – yet it's perfectly safe
and checked every day.

Reader 2: In many countries only a minority have access to clean
water.

Reader 3: In India only a third of the nation gets clean water. In
Indonesia alone over a hundred million people do not get
guaranteed safe water.

Reader 4: In Afghanistan only one in ten families has safe
water.

Reader 1: So as you wake up each morning remember the army
on the move. . . .

Reader 2: Every day new taps are installed and slowly the battle is being won – governments, the World Bank, charities and the people themselves are all helping.

Christian Aid

Christian Aid's address is: Christian Aid, PO Box 1, London SW9 8BH.

The Ascension and Whitsun

Forty days after Easter the Christian Church celebrates the Ascension, when Christ in his transfigured, glorified body left his Apostles and returned to heaven. Ten days later comes Pentecost – the Greek word for 'fifty' because Pentecost is fifty days after Easter. Ths is the day of the Confirmation of the Apostles when they received the gift of the Holy Spirit and when the Church was really born. Pentecost was once a favourite feast for the Baptism of new Christians and, as they wore white garments, this feast has also come to be called Whit Sunday. Two other great feasts follow soon afterwards. Corpus Christi, when Catholics celebrate Christ's real presence still among them, and the Sacred Heart, when they honour the great love of their Saviour.

Peter Kelly

One of the wonderful sights of springtime is the bursting forth of blossom on a fruit tree. This sight lasts for a relatively short time, and is not repeated through the summer. It would, however, be a mistaken desire to wish for a fruit tree that was always attractively in blossom; for its purpose is to bear fruit. But in addition to its manifest beauty, the blossom is, in its place, of great value as a witness. It reveals the presence of creative life; and it is the promise of subsequent fruit.

Similarly on the day of Pentecost, seven weeks after Christ's resurrection from the dead, and ten days after his ascension, something happened among the company of Christ's followers which not only arrested attention, and made men stop to look and to listen, but which also had great significance as a witness to important and far-reaching spiritual truths. On the one hand, it was a sign of vital fulfilment; it revealed that the spirit of Jesus was alive and active to do and to teach. On the other hand, it was a promise of all-embracing enlargement – of fruit-bearing in every member, and of effective witness-bearing among every nation under heaven.

A.M. Stibbs

Luke, chapter 24, verses 50–3 *describe the Ascension; and* Acts, chapter 2 *tells the story of the first 'Whit Sunday', a day Christians regard as marking the birthday of the church.*

Ramadan

A passage to mark the Muslim month of fasting, or to be used as a comparison with the Christian season of Lent.

A central Muslim duty is to observe the fast that lasts for the whole of the Islamic month of Ramadan. Due to the nature of the lunar Islamic calendar, Ramadan circulates through every season of our solar year. During Ramadan it is forbidden to eat, drink or partake of any form of enjoyment, even down to smelling perfume, between the hours of sunrise and sunset. In Islamic countries a cannon may be fired to signal the start and end of each day's fast. It is remarkable in an Islamic city, as evening comes during Ramadan, to hear the boom of the cannon and see the streets come to life, the restaurants fill up and the sudden air of chatter and gaiety. At the end of the month there is a celebration, with feasting and fireworks. There is a special duty to give to the poor to celebrate the end of Ramadan.

People who are ill, travelling or serving as soldiers in wartime are freed from the duties of Ramadan, although they should try to fast at some other time of the year instead. Pregnant and nursing mothers are exempt altogether. The fast commemorates the Prophet's first vision. It is known that he experienced it during the month of Ramadan but not on what day: therefore the whole month must be observed. . . .

When the Prophet was about twenty-five, it was his custom to wander in the mountains and in the blazing heat of the desert to try to make contact with God. He searched for many years with no result. Then, when he was aged about forty, he experienced his first vision. He heard strange noises and voices muttering around him in the desert. Full of fear, he hid in a mountain cave. There, the tradition goes, he felt the Angel Gabriel (a figure belonging also in Jewish and Christian lore) seize him with great force and utter the command: 'Proclaim!' Then God engraved upon his mind the earliest verses of the Koran.

Colin Cross

The Hajj

1: TO MECCA

The date of the hajj *varies from year to year.*

The *hajj* is the fifth pillar of Islam. A Muslim must believe in one
God – 'there is no God but Allah and Mohammed is His Messenger'. (This does not rule out respect for the major Old and
New Testament figures. They classify as prophets and men of
God, although not of the same standing as Mohammed.) He
must pray five times daily, facing Mecca. He must pay alms to the
needy at two and a half per cent of his income. He must fast from
sunset to sunrise during Ramadan.

At least once in his life, money and health permitting, he must
make the *hajj* to Mecca, in Saudi Arabia.

The rites of the *hajj* revolve around Abraham. After he had a
son, Ismael, by the slave girl Hagar, Abraham was forced by his
wife Sarah to abandon both mother and child. He left them by the
ruins of the first Ka'ba, the House of God.

The Ka'ba is set with a black stone, the *Hajar al-Aswan*, perhaps
of meteoric origin. Gabriel is said to have given it to Abraham.

Searching desperately for water in the desert, Hagar ran seven
times between two brown hills, Al-Safa and Al-Marwa. Muslims
believe that the Lord gave Abraham a lamb to slaughter in place
of his son at Mina, not far from Mecca.

The pilgrims arrive in their thousands, spilling out of jets and
rusting Red Sea steamers. A special Saudi Ministry tries to cope
with tented cities, water points and field hospitals. Many old men
deliberately expose themselves to the sun in the hope of dying in
such a holy place.

An army of *mutawifs*, pilgrim guides, herds them and profits
from them. The *mutawif* gets them through quarantine at the

docks or airport, ferries them in buses, cashes their drafts, crowds them into his dormitories and feeds them from his kitchens. He sells them broiler chickens and Pepsi (no Coke – it's sold in Israel) and, when they buy consecrated sheep – for slaughter at double the market price – the *mutawif* is the middleman.

Pilgrimage is as booming a business as any in Saudi Arabia. In 1938, just 108,000 pilgrims were recorded. This year the figure will be around two million.

Brian Moynahan

(N.B. see also pages 141–2).

2: THE KA'BA

On entering Mecca, the believer heads straight for the Ka'ba, fighting his way through the dense throng to the Black Stone, which he tries to kiss, 'an act that will give him heavenly delight'; if he cannot get close enough he touches it with his staff. He is required to make seven circuits of the Ka'ba, the first three with a leaping gait, touching the Black Stone each time round.

The pilgrim must then race seven times between two little holy mounds set nearly half a mile apart, repeating all the while verses from the Koran and other pious formulae. Only then can he leave Mecca for his vigil at Arafat, the essential moment.

There follows a mad dusk stampede – in which every year there are fatal accidents – to yet another holy place for a further vigil, and then on before sunrise to the village of Mina, where the final gory ceremonies of the *hajj* take place.

At Mina, within the space of a few hours, several hundred thousand consecrated sheep have their throats cut as their heads are made to face the Ka'ba. The sacrifice overflows the slaughter-house into the street. The sand is stained like a medieval battlefield. Some of the meat is eaten by the pilgrims and some is distributed among the poor, but most of the carcass is left lying on the ground. There are just not enough poor. After about twenty-four hours the army moves in and starts cleaning up.

After the sacrifice, the pilgrim puts himself into the hands of a barber, who shaves his head and cuts his nails. This bodily waste is carefully buried. The pilgrim then returns to Mecca, circles the Ka'ba a few times and, thus desanctified, completes his pilgrimage. If he has any money left after having run the gauntlet of guides, taxi-drivers, keepers of historic houses and pedlars of all sorts, he may then enjoy the pleasures of the city free from all taboos.

He will finally return home filled with tremendous joy. He will be proud to be a soldier in the vast army of the faithful.

Patrick Seale

Summer holiday

It was at Whitley Bay that my Uncle Hal failed to teach me to swim.

I had never much wanted to swim, because the waves splashed my glasses, but my old Aunt Emma thought no lad should grow up without being able to rescue the cat if a dam burst. There was no dam in six counties but she had read about one bursting in America and she argued that everything that hit America arrived in Britain shortly afterwards; it was something to do with the Gulf Stream. Every time she read that New York was blanketed in snow, I had to go out in extra combinations.

Uncle Hal hadn't wanted to go to Whitley Bay either, as it was Thursday, the day he took his wireless to pieces, but Aunt Emma insisted; he was the best man qualified to teach me to swim, she said, because of his experience as a temporary Turkish baths attendant during the engineers' lockout.

Aunt Emma stood guard over a sand dune while I changed into my green bathing costume. She had knitted it herself; it had one long leg to keep the cold out of my bad knee, which had been kicked by a cow during a football match down by the Gut. (The cows won one nowt.) Then I dashed furtively down to the sea.

I was splashing in ten inches of water when Uncle Hal came up behind me with his trousers rolled up, seized my head and held it under the waves. This was the best way, he explained afterwards, to overcome my fear of water.

There were several seconds during which I saw myself not growing up to be a window cleaner or left half for Newcastle United. Then I lashed out and kicked Uncle Hal in the stomach. At the same time, a dog which was fetching a stick for a man grew excited by the commotion, and bit my uncle in the calf.

209

They brought my old Aunt Emma and she stood guard over me while Uncle Hal and the man went into the sand dune.

On the way home, we got off the bus at Dr Duncan's and explained to him that Uncle Hal had been kicked in the stomach and bitten by a dog while holding my head under the sea. Dr Duncan said, yes, there was a lot of it about and handed my uncle some ointment for the black eye the man had given him.

I never overcame my fear of Whitley Bay. What's more, my old Aunt Emma's trepidation about America communicated itself to me.

To this day, I never read about potato blight scourging Montana without thinking it might be swept across here on the Gulf Stream and start attacking human beings.

Leonard Barras

PRAYERS AND
THOUGHTS

Prayers and thoughts

The Lord's Prayer

Our Father, who art in heaven,
hallowed be thy name;
thy kingdom come;
thy will be done;
on earth as it is in heaven.
Give us this day our daily bread.
And forgive us our trespasses,
as we forgive those who trespass against us.
And lead us not into temptation;
but deliver us from evil.

For thine is the kingdom, the power, and the glory,
for ever and ever.   Amen.

The Lord's Prayer (*Alternative Service Book*)

Our Father in heaven
hallowed be your name,
your kingdom come,
your will be done,
on earth as in heaven.
Give us today our daily bread.
Forgive us our sins
as we forgive those who sin against us.
Lead us not into temptation
but deliver us from evil.

For the kingdom, the power, and the glory are yours
now and forever.   Amen.

213

The prayer for God's presence

Into thy hands, O Lord
we commend ourselves this day.
Let thy presence be with us to its close.
Help us to see that in doing our work we are doing thy will,
and that by serving others we are serving thee,
through Jesus Christ our Lord.   Amen.

The prayer for purity

Almighty God, unto whom all hearts be open
all desires known,
and from whom no secrets are hid.
Cleanse the thoughts of our hearts
by the inspiration of thy Holy Spirit,
that we may perfectly love thee,
and worthily magnify thy holy Name
through Christ our Lord.   Amen.

The prayer for today

O Lord, our heavenly Father,
Almighty and everlasting God
who hast safely brought us to the beginning of this day,
defend us in the same with thy mighty power,
and grant that this day we fall into no sin
neither run into any kind of danger,
but that all our doings may be ordered by thy governance,
to do always that is righteous in thy sight,
through Jesus Christ our Lord.   Amen.

The prayer for all men

O heavenly Father,
we pray thee to send into our hearts and into the hearts
    of all men everywhere,
the Spirit of our Lord Jesus Christ.   Amen.

214

The prayer of St Ignatius Loyola

Teach us, good Lord
to serve thee as thou deservest,
to give and not to count the cost,
to fight and not to heed the wounds,
to toil and not to seek for rest,
to labour and not to ask for any reward,
save that of knowing that we do thy will.   Amen.

A prayer of St Richard

Praise be to thee, O Lord Jesus Christ,
for all the benefits which thou has given us,
for all the pains and insults
thou has borne for me;
O most merciful Redeemer,
Friend and Brother,
may we know thee more clearly,
love thee more dearly,
and follow thee more nearly.   Amen.

The prayer of St Francis

Lord, make us instruments of thy peace.
Where there is hatred, let us sow love;
Where there is injury, pardon;
Where there is discord, union;
Where there is doubt, faith;
Where there is despair, hope;
Where there is darkness, light;
Where there is sadness, joy;
For thy mercy and for thy truth's sake.

Grant that we may not seek so much to be consoled, as to
    console;
To be understood, as to understand;
To be loved, as to love.
For it is in giving that we receive;
    in pardoning we are pardoned;
    and in dying, we are born to eternal life.   Amen.

The Mool Mantra

There is one God.
Eternal Truth is His name:
Maker of all things, immanent in all things.
Fearing nothing and at enmity with nothing.
Timeless is His image;
Not begotten, being of His own being:
By the grace of the Guru, made known to men.

The Guru Granth Sahib opens with these words, which enshrine the Sikh doctrine of God. In abbreviated form they are often to be seen written on the canopy which is erected over the throne of the sacred book.

The words constitute the Mool Mantra or basic, or perfect mantra. A mantra is a sacred chant often passed like a secret from a guru to his disciple.

The Exordium

(The opening words of the Quran)

IN THE NAME OF GOD
THE COMPASSIONATE
THE MERCIFUL

Praise be to God, Lord of the Creation,
The Compassionate, the Merciful,
King of Judgement Day!
You alone we worship, and to You alone
we pray for help.
Guide us to the straight path
The path of those whom You have favoured,
Not of these who have incurred Your wrath,
Nor of those who have gone astray.

A Hindu hymn

Praise to you, O Trinity,
    one before creation,
afterwards divided
    in your three qualities.

In the cycle of your day and night
    all things live and all things die
But when you wake we live,
    when you sleep we perish.

You are the knower and the known,
  you are the eater and the food,
you are the priest and the oblation,
  you are the worshipper and the prayer.

(Kalidasa : Kumarasam/bhava)

Jewish prayers

Men of Israel, listen: God, our Lord is one:
  he alone is our God:
We bless his name:
His Kingdom will last for ever and ever.

We bless the Lord by day:
We bless the Lord by night:
We bless the Lord when we go to bed:
We bless the Lord when we wake up.

We know that he who looks after Israel
Never sleeps.

We trust our souls to your hands, O Lord.
You have saved us, Lord God of truth.

We put our hope, O Lord, in your help and power.

(from the Authorised Daily Prayer Book*)*

Hare Krishna

Hare Krishna,
Krishna, Krishna.
Hare Hare,
Hare Rama
Hare Rama
Rama Rama
Hare Hare.

Recitation of mantras, *particularly this one, is a yogic process. Yoga, from which is derived the English word 'yoke', means to join or link with God, and thus be relieved of the excessively materialistic pressures which characterize our time. The Sanskrit word* Hara *is the form of addressing the energy of Almighty God. This word denotes the supreme pleasure energy of the Lord.* Hara *is changed to the vocative* Hare *in the* mantra. *The recitation or singing of the* mahamantra *is a spiritual call for God and his energy. The words* Krishna *and* Rama *are forms of directly addressing the Lord himself.*

217

A prayer for unity

Sovereign Lord, Creator of our plural
   and multi-racial society,
Redeemer of our sins of racism,
   by your Holy Spirit
guide us towards racial understanding, justice and peace.
This we ask in the name of God.   Amen.

Prayers for schools

Almighty God, we beseech thee with thy gracious favour to behold our universities, colleges and schools, that knowledge may be increased among us, and all good learning flourish and abound. Bless all who teach and all who learn; and grant that in humility of heart they may ever look unto thee, who art the foundation of all wisdom.   Amen.

Prosper with thy blessing, O Lord, the work of this school, and grant that those who serve thee here may set thy holy will ever before them, doing that which is well-pleasing in thy sight and persevering in thy service unto the end.   Amen.

O Almighty God, who has gathered us together as members of one body, grant that we may realize our responsibility to one another; may truth, honour and kindness abound amongst us; may thy blessing rest upon our work, may thy Name be hallowed in our midst, and thy peace guard our hearts.   Amen.

Index